The Hunter's Book of the Whitetail

NORTH★AMERICAN★HUNTING★CLUB

THE HUNTER'S BOOK
OF THE WHITETAIL

Text by Ron Spomer
Photography by Michael Francis

NORTH★AMERICAN★HUNTING★CLUB

Minnetonka, Minnesota

ABOUT THE AUTHOR

A widely published writer and outdoor photographer since 1976, Ron Spomer has explored, hunted, fished, camped and photographed in 40 states and 5 countries from the Arctic Circle to South Africa. As a former public relations officer with two conservation agencies and naturalist with wide interests, he has written about subjects as diverse as hunting, fishing, bird watching, wildlife art, protecting wetlands and perpetuating dwindling wildlife diversity on island habitats.

His work has been published in more than 100 magazines from *Wing & Shot* to *Audubon*. He is Rifles columnist for *Sporting Classics* magazine, a technical writer at *Rifle* magazine and a regular contributor to *American Hunter* and *Rifle & Shotgun* magazines.

Spomer is the author/photographer of *The Rut*, a comparative study of North American big game animal behavior; *Big Game Hunter's Guide to Montana*; and co-author of *Advanced Whitetail Hunting*. He has served as editor for two other hunting books. When not afield Spomer divides his time between homes in Idaho and Indiana.

ABOUT THE PHOTOGRAPHER

Michael H. Francis, born in Maine, has spent the past thirty years as a resident of Montana. Mike is a graduate of Montana State University. Previous to becoming a full-time photographer, he worked seasonally in Yellowstone National Park for 15 seasons.

Mike's photography has been internationally recognized for its beautiful and informative nature imagery. His work has been published by the National Geographic Society, The Audubon Society, The National Wildlife Federation, and *North American Hunter*, *Field & Stream* and *Outdoor Life* magazines, among others.

He has photographed more than 15 books including *Track of the Coyote*, *Mule Deer Country*, *Elk Country*, *Wild Sheep Country* and *Moose*.

Mike lives in Billings, Montana, with his family.

THE HUNTER'S BOOK OF THE WHITETAIL

Printed in 2006.

TOM CARPENTER
Creative Director

HEATHER KOSHIOL
Book Development Coordinator

SHARI GROSS
Production Assistant

PATRICIA BICKNER LINDER
Book Design and Production

DAN KENNEDY
Photo Editor

Drawings © Patricia Bickner Linder

PHOTO CREDITS:
All photos © Michael H. Francis except: page 4 Mark & Sue Werner; 20 Cabela's; 41 © Birkhead, M. OSF/Animals Animals; 42 © Peter Baumann/Animals Animals; 43 © Darek Karp/Animals Animals; 44 (top) © Stefan Myers/Animals Animals; 44 (bottom) © Darek Karp/Animals Animals; 46 (top) © Richard Shiell/Animals Animals; 46 (bottom) © Michael Dick/Animals Animals; 118, 119 John Ford.

8 9 10 11 12 13 / 10 09 08 07 06 05
ISBN 1-58159-076-8
© 2000 North American Hunting Club

North American Hunting Club
12301 Whitewater Drive
Minnetonka, MN 55343
www.huntingclub.com

PHOTOGRAPHER'S ACKNOWLEDGEMENTS

Through the years I've photographed most of North America's large game for book projects, but never have I traveled so extensively as for this project. White-tailed deer have taken me from the top of Maine to the tip of Florida, from the Upper Peninsula of Michigan to the Rio Grande of Texas, through wheat fields, badlands, and the mountain foothills of the Rocky Mountain West. Seems like everywhere I go I see whitetails! Would you believe I even saw a whitetail in the Yukon Territory of Canada?

This has been a long project and a number of people have unselfishly extended me their help and guidance. I would like to thank some of those folks now.

My wife, Victoria, and daughters, Elizabeth and Emily, rarely are able to accompany me on photo trips. I truly appreciate their willingness to stay home and encourage me from afar.

Special thanks goes to my friend Mark Werner and his wife Sue. Mark, a fellow wildlife photographer, unselfishly guided me to many of his "secret" whitetail hot spots in the Midwest. Without his help and guidance, I would have had a much harder time photographing secret deer behavior.

Many other kind people have helped me along the way with this project including: Lee Greenly, James A. McAllen and family, Bill Silliker Jr., Steve Antus and Steven G. Maka. Thanks to all of you for your contributions to this book project.

The white-tailed deer have very special friends in John Jorstad, Stan & Ester Stevenson and Dave Satre. Thanks for sharing your animal friends with me.

—Michael H. Francis

TABLE OF CONTENTS

FOREWORD 9

INTRODUCTION   **THIS WONDROUS WHITETAIL** 11
AMERICA'S DEER 13

CHAPTER ONE   **ORIGINS & EVOLUTION** 25
HOW DEER CAME TO BE 27
THE WORLD'S LIVING DEER 41

CHAPTER TWO   **ANATOMY** 51
PREDATOR DEFENSES 53
PELAGE 70
DIGESTIVE SYSTEM 74
COMMUNICATIONS 82
ANTLERS 93

CHAPTER THREE   **BEHAVIOR & SEASONS** 129
THE SPRING FLING 131
IN THE GOOD OLD SUMMERTIME 144
AUTUMN SPLENDOR 159
HANGING ON—WINTER 178

FOREWORD

Whitetail hunters love the white-tailed deer. Nonhunters often can't comprehend that fact— that we can so admire and respect the animal we are pursuing. But for those of us fortunate enough to be in the whitetail woods every autumn, our love for whitetails is a fact of life.

There aren't enough adjectives to describe the whitetail perfectly and completely. Smart. Shy. Reclusive. Beautiful. Elusive. Thrilling. Fast. Heart-stopping. Graceful. They're only words, and they only *begin* to put together a picture of what a whitetail is and what he means to a hunter.

That's why we at the North American Hunting Club created *The Hunter's Book of the Whitetail*—to take you, in words *and* pictures, right into whitetail country and create for you some of the heart-thumping feelings you generate deep down inside when a real whitetail steps into view.

Yes, this book will help you appreciate whitetails and understand even more about their very nature and lifestyle. That in itself is worthwhile. But our idea is to teach you some things about whitetail behavior as well. And if it all helps you become a more successful hunter, all the better. We make no apologies there: this is a book *by* hunters, *for* hunters.

The best in the business helped us pull together all these pictures and words: Michael Francis behind the camera, traveling across whitetail range from north to south and east to west; and Ron Spomer pulling together words that have a way of entertaining while informing you.

The whitetail is everyone's deer. It doesn't matter how much money you have or what you drive or where you live or whether you hunt with gun, bow or both…if you love whitetails and love to hunt them, then this book will hold some meaning for you.

INTRODUCTION

THIS
WONDROUS
WHITETAIL

AMERICA'S DEER

Compared to most deer, the whitetail doesn't look too impressive. The 1,400-pound moose, with antlers spreading 7 feet, towers over it. The elk, with 6-foot antler beams and 2-foot tines, appears much more regal. And the caribou, migrating across desolate tundra beneath a maze of antler palms and tines, looks alluringly exotic. Even the blocky mule deer, with its tall, wide antlers, seems more majestic against its background of snow-capped mountains. But none of that matters, because here in America when you say whitetail, you've said *deer*. The whitetail is our antlered prototype, first among equals, symbol of American wilderness forests, farmland fields and suburban meadows. It's the boss buck. King stag. The deer we love.

Our ordinary whitetail is Everyman's deer; the common, red-blooded, hot-dogs-and-apple-pie, all-American backyard deer from Maine to Washington and from Florida to Arizona.

Opposite page: A Texas whitetail buck at sunrise surveys his domain. The whitetail is America's most widely distributed deer, commonly found from Maine to Washington and from Florida to Arizona.

Adapting to man's encroachment has not been a problem for whitetails. In fact, in many localities deer have become backyard nuisances, ravaging gardens, rubbing saplings and spreading unwanted pellets in manicured yards.

It's as accessible to a young couple living in a mobile home as it is to a retired millionaire living on a private estate. It prowls wild north woods and southern swamps, yet is usually the first large wild animal most Americans see; sometimes it's the only one. While other big mammals shy away from encroaching civilization, the whitetail thumbs its nose at humans and persists. It has adapted to life on the edge of suburbia, foraging on cemeteries and golf courses, even hiding inside large city parks. This isn't just a deer; it's the American wilderness wrapped in a sleek brown package, tied with a flashy white ribbon and sent daily to remind us where we've been and warn us against where we are heading.

PRACTICAL HERO

Beyond wilderness icon, the whitetail is also a national hero. For thousands of years it provided Native Americans with sustenance, clothing, shelter and tools. More than any other animal, it fed the pilgrims, fostered development of the long rifle and honed the shootin' eyes of the colonists who won our freedom from King George. The whitetail lured Daniel Boone across the Appalachians and helped fuel Lewis and Clark up the Missouri. Many a pioneer family pulled through lean times on the flesh of whitetails. Even today, with suburbs and highways spreading at a frightening rate, whitetails still dash through our woods, forage in our fields, grace our dinner tables and haunt our autumn dreams.

Like the early Americans who depended on them, whitetails are tough, energetic, resilient, adaptable and self-sufficient. Unlike modern Americans, they are not ready to capitulate to all-out development. They resist encroaching concrete. After the sun has set and we've retired to the security of our houses, theaters and bars, whitetails gambol from forests and woods, thickets and swamps, ditches and sloughs, dragging wilderness onto our carefully tended fields and lawns. While we sleep, they raid cornfields, ravage manicured shrubbery, rub sapling shade trees, trample gardens and spread pellets of discord. They seem to say, *You may have destroyed the passenger pigeon, nearly wiped out the bison and whooping crane, but we're still here. And we're staying, no matter what you do to the land.*

ATHLETE EXTRAORDINAIRE

Much of the whitetail's mystique revolves around its remarkable physical abilities. Anyone who startles a whitetail at close range marvels at both the speed with which it dashes away and the fluid grace with which it soars over logs and limbs. More than one frustrated gardener has raised a 6-foot fence to 8 feet to protect his produce from marauding deer, only to stand fuming and dumbfounded when a mere slip of a doe calmly takes her measure of the high wire, coils, then leaps over. During organized drives to chase semi-tame deer from holding pens, biologists have seen the animals clear 9½-foot fences. This seems all the more amazing when you realize that it's done without weight training, steroids or practice. Odds are the first 9-foot fence any whitetail clears is the first it ever tried to clear. Imagine what they could leap with Olympic coaching.

In the 100-yard dash and cross-country run the whitetail is equally impressive. Normally, deer walk at a leisurely 3½ to 4 miles per hour, their vegetative prey requiring no faster approach. In fact, a slow, cautious deer is a safe deer because it has time to sniff, look and listen for predators. Unless under imminent attack, slow and steady wins the race.

Yet when cougar, wolf or man presses hard upon the whitetail's life, it explodes away at 20, 30 or even 40 miles per hour. Again, no training, very little practice, just jump-and-run. Lest you think this no big accomplishment, try running flat out at dusk through a young forest, uphill and down, dodging trees and leaping fallen logs. You'll either modify your opinion or break your neck. It is the whitetail's agility at top speed that makes it a world-class athlete extraordinaire.

Despite their bold taunting, or perhaps because of it, we admire them, respect them, even love them. Here is a creature with the temerity to rest calmly in an interstate highway ditch, chewing cud without losing a shred of dignity, even as 40,000-pound trucks thunder past. It parades nonchalantly past barking dogs lunging at chain-link fences. When bulldozers move in, it waits patiently just beyond the carnage, then returns after the nurseryman sets out the new shrubbery. While tractors churn the fields, it bides its time in the woods until the wheat sprouts or the corn ripens. At the same time it maintains the nobility and self-sufficiency to live quietly in the most pristine wilderness. And while hunters prowl autumn woods and fields, it lies flat among barnyard pig weed, sleeps amid lilacs behind school playgrounds unseen (and often unsuspected), until one November night when a businessman driving home from the office collides with a buck no one has ever seen before: its antlers thick as a bat handle, wide as a recliner and tall as a kid's tricycle with enough tines and points to hang a load of laundry.

LANGUAGE LESSONS

The whitetail is such an integral part of our national consciousness that it has become part of the language. The buck that was sold by market hunters for one dollar became the paper "buck" in our wallets. A summer group of bachelor whitetails became the perfect metaphor for a "stag" party. We instantly recognize the simple innocence of a "doe-eyed" young girl, or the indecision of someone "frozen like a deer in the headlights." The erect tail of a fleeing whitetail certainly inspired the phrase "hightailing it" to describe a hasty departure. And even though we may never have personally handled a fawn, we know what someone means when they say "gentle as a fawn."

The stereotypical backwoods village must be Bucksnort Junction, and nearly every state has a whitetail or flagtail creek, lake, ridge, peak, valley or slough. Virtually any short, wild shrubbery is known colloquially as buckbrush. From Florida to Washington, whitetails truly have branded America.

For more proof that whitetails are integral to our society, look carefully at Christmas decorations depicting Santa's reindeer. Often they look more like whitetails than caribou. Notice also plastic and concrete lawn statues of whitetail "families," the regal buck standing guard over his inanimate doe and fawns. Minnesota, Wisconsin and Texas towns even erect dinosaur-sized statues of leaping whitetails in honor of the deer's contribution to the local culture and economy. Whitetail images adorn mailboxes and stationery, beer cans and thermometers. Landscape painters often insert whitetails into their scenes, whether of northwoods lake shore, Rocky Mountain peak or Sonoran desert saguaro forest. Major corporations even hitch their reputations to whitetails—"Nothing runs like a Deere."

SHOW ME THE MONEY

Not surprisingly, the whitetail's notoriety and allure have made it an economic powerhouse. Although market hunting for venison has long been outlawed, whitetail

Opposite page: This doe has done a good job raising her twin fawns through the spring, summer and fall. Next comes the real test: winter.

HISTORIC USES

J ust as poor pioneers used every part of a pig but the squeal, so did Indians use every part of a whitetail but the snort. This was their general store on the hoof, the original Mall of America.

From deer, innovative natives made shirts, pants, shoes, gloves, hats, pouches, blankets, quivers, harnesses, snowshoe webbing, shields, arm guards, tepees, saddle pads, thongs, laces and balls for game playing. This was just from the hides.

Sinew was turned into thread, bowstrings and fishnets. Bones were made into hide fleshers and scrapers, hoes, shovels and digging sticks, flutes, fish hooks, clubs, spear and arrow points, needles and awls, arrow straighteners, jewelry and spoons. Antlers were fashioned into deadly club points, arrow, harpoon and spear heads, needles, flaking tools for working flint and obsidian, combs, orna-ments, knife handles, whistles, drumsticks and rattles.

Gut was used to store tallow, string bows and sew leather. Hooves were strung together to make rattles or boiled to make glue. Toothed jaws rasped dried corn off cobs. Fat seasoned and preserved food, helped soften tanned hides, oiled hair, greased swimmers and wrestlers, protected sensitive skin (the original Chap-Stick), and served as a general lubricant. Face masks were worn in ceremonial dances and as decoys for stalking more deer. Even the whitetail's hair was woven and embroidered into garments and ceremonial head gear.

For thousands of years, early Americans were largely dependent on whitetails for their subsistence. And almost all internal organs were eaten too, including the nearly digested vegetation from the small intestines and lower stomach—reportedly the only food a starving human could keep down.

flesh and hides still pull in millions each year—in license dollars that fund conservation around the country. Because many states lump whitetail permit sales with mule deer and other big game, exact numbers for whitetail tags alone are not known, but it has been estimated that nearly 10 million sportsmen stalk this species each year. Assign a conservative average of $20 per license (some resident permits sell for less than $10, some nonresident tags run as high as $750), and our favorite deer is worth $200 million in the U.S. alone. Add more for Canada and Mexico. That dollar amount is nothing to sneeze at, but it doesn't begin to cover the real value of venison. Figure a low average of 50 pounds of lean red meat per harvested deer, multiply that by about 4 million whitetails harvested each year, and you have 200 million pounds of low-fat, low-cholesterol food. At just $2 per pound that venison is worth $400 million. But that's not all. There are all those hides that get sold and converted into hundreds of thousands of buckskin gloves, vests and jackets. And the antlers: These days trophy-sized racks fetch thousands of dollars. Even replicas of record-sized antlers rake in as much as $10,000 each.

STUFF, STUFF & MORE STUFF

But the real money flows from ancillary products and services that hunters purchase—guns and bows, cartridges and arrows, binoculars and scopes, boots and hats, camouflage pants and Gore-Tex jackets. Dozens of small companies and hundreds of mom-and-pop operations manufacture and sell treestands, ground blinds, seat cushions, grunt calls, fake rattling antlers, compasses, GPS units, game bags, skinning knives, gland scents and lures, decoys and drag ropes. The Idaho Fish & Game Department tallied what Gem State hunters spend for their deer hunts and came up

Opposite page: Some towns honor their namesake with huge statues such as this one in Deerwood, Minnesota. Above: About 4 million whitetails are harvested each year by nearly 10 million hunters who give life to small-town and rural economies.

It's estimated that Americans spend a total of $10.3 billion a year on deer hunting. Everyone seems to love deer—and as a result, our economy benefits.

with an average value of $4,000 per deer. That's probably an underestimate. The designing and marketing of new camouflage patterns alone is worth millions annually. Then there are audio and video tapes and CDs, how-to books and magazines, cookbooks, taxidermy supplies, sleeping bags, tents and stoves, portable radios, four-wheel drive vehicles and their array of backcountry accoutrements. The list of expenses related to whitetail hunting goes on and on, sometimes even including the costs of diamond rings and, if those don't work, divorce lawyers.

And don't forget about all the folk—north, south, east and west—who make at least part of their living from guiding and outfitting whitetail hunters.

What does it all add up to? Southwick Associates, a fish and wildlife economics and business consulting firm, compiled numbers for one deer hunting season that totaled $10.3 billion in retail sales for goods and services purchased by U.S. deer hunters. That included blacktail and mule deer hunters, but the vast majority was spent by whitetail hunters. The multiplier effect of these sales—that is, the total cash transactions from buyer to supplier to manufacturer to workers resulting from the sale

of each piece of equipment—exceeded $27.8 billion. Taxes generated, including sales tax and income taxes created by the multiplier effect, added up to nearly $1.5 billion.

And we're still not finished. Nonhunters also sacrificed at the altar of the whitetail. From Texas ranchers to New Jersey suburbanites, folks buy and maintain elaborate feeders and stock them with expensive grains. They purchase high-dollar binoculars, cameras and camcorders to document their sightings. Some take vacations halfway across the country to view or photograph whitetails. Many collect whitetail art prints, bronze sculptures and plates. They wear whitetail T-shirts and caps. According to the U.S. Department of Commerce and the U.S. Department of Interior, 76 million Americans spend $18 billion on so-called nonconsumptive wildlife recreation in one year. Much of this is bird watching and exotic trips to see caribou in Alaska, no doubt, but if we credit the popular whitetail with inspiring just 10 percent of this activity, which seems reasonable given its broad appeal, the total is a whopping $1.8 billion. If whitetails were Whitetails, Inc., they would turn a profit in excess of $12 billion in one year. General Motors, the largest automobile manufacturer in the world, comes up with only about $5 billion in profit in one year.

One economic downside to whitetails: Farmers lose millions of dollars every year in crop depredation wrought by deer.

OVERHEAD

Of course there is an economic downside to whitetails, too. Call it production overhead: things like crop depredation and automobile collisions. Although nationwide figures are not available, numbers from individual states provide some idea of the magnitude. In recent years Pennsylvania has estimated agricultural damage from whitetails at more than $100 million annually. Wisconsin pays out about $1.5

*Where crops are
available, whitetails use
them extensively.*

million annually to farmers in compensation for crop losses to deer, but actual damages are much higher, averaging more than $40 million. Damage assessments on individual farms have come in as high as $40,000. Damages to suburban lawns and park vegetation aren't even calculated, nor is destruction of critical nesting habitat for dozens of other animal species, some of them endangered. Overpopulations of whitetails threaten to wipe out some endangered plants in the eastern states.

In several midwest states commercial crops constitute 50 percent of forage consumed by whitetails. In Iowa 70 percent of a whitetail's diet by weight is corn. Biologists in Wisconsin estimate that if deer hunting were stopped and whitetails left to multiply unchecked, they would drive the state's farmers out of business within 5 years. Similar tragedy would befall nearly every other state where humans grow vegetables, for whitetails and crops are virtually inseparable. From tomatoes to squash, potatoes to Christmas trees, whitetails will eat almost anything. Hunting as a means to control the deer population is critical for protecting agriculture. Ironically, even many organic farmers must shoot depredating deer in order to provide vegetables for animal rights activists.

Obviously, the whitetail is more than just a deer. It's a major force in American life. It's an economic powerhouse, a catalyst for industry, a source of food and clothing, impetus for recreation, inspiration for millions and a major predator of agricultural crops. More importantly it's a symbol of America: independent, free and persevering. Part myth, part mystery, part majesty, part hope and part promise. And a whole lot of yearning. Whitetails are part of us, part of our past and part of our future. Long may they thrive.

HISTORIC POPULATIONS

Now that whitetails have reached pest status in many regions, hunters often boast that deer number more now than before the coming of European settlers. The best current estimates put the U.S. whitetail herd at between 17 and 25 million. Were historic numbers higher?

Sixteenth-century explorers like de Soto, Coronado and Gorges described deer in abundance from Florida to Texas to Maine. In October of 1621, Wampanoag Indians invited to a Puritan Thanksgiving despaired at the paucity of food, so they slipped into the woods and in short order killed enough venison to feed 140 hearty appetites. During a 1728 French military campaign against the Fox Indians in Wisconsin, natives allied with the French secured sufficient venison during one hunt to supply 1,400 men for several days.

Decade after decade throughout the 1800s, pioneers remarked on the abundance of deer as they pushed into virgin country. During the 19th century, various naturalists reported whitetail densities from 100 per square mile in New England to 58 per square mile in Indiana and 25 per square mile in parts of Wisconsin. Even in mature hardwood/conifer forests in the Great Lakes region there were 10 to 15 per square mile. After consulting hundreds of such historic accounts, turn-of-the-century naturalist Earnest Thompson Seton estimated that an average of 20 whitetails per square mile swarmed across 2 million square miles of habitat from the Mississippi River Valley east to the Atlantic. That adds up to 40 million. Throw in another million acres of habitat west of the Mississippi at an ultraconservative density of 5 per square mile, and the total balloons to 45 million.

Another way to calculate whitetail abundance is to determine historic Native American use and harvest. Middens (ancient trash dumps) uncovered in West Virginia revealed that whitetails made up almost 90 percent of all animal meat consumed by a village of 500 to 1000 people. A similar percentage was found in a Connecticut site. Even at a fishing camp in New York, discarded bones indicated whitetails constituted 55 percent of the ancient angler's meat diet, bullhead catfish 15 percent and black bears another 15 percent.

It is generally accepted that about 2.3 million Native Americans lived in traditional whitetail range before Europeans settled the area. If we figure a daily consumption of 2 pounds of animal food per person each day, just 25 percent of it venison, Natives would have killed between 4.6 and 6.4 million whitetails each year. To support that level of harvest plus losses to wolves, cougars and other historically abundant predators, the deer population had to have been at least 14 to 20 million. But, considering the higher percentages of whitetail bones found in middens, it is more likely Natives were annually withdrawing closer to 12 million deer from a bank of 25 to 35 million, possibly 40 million.

Another way to test these numbers is to examine the wardrobe of the period. Based on traditional Native dress (6 hides per man, 8 per woman, fewer for children) lasting an average of two years, each person would have required about 3.45 new whitetail hides annually, necessitating an annual collection of just over 8 million deer. In order to sustain that kind of harvest, there had to have been at least 25 million whitetails roaming the woods.

We will never know the exact number of whitetails that graced the pristine North American landscape, but somewhere between 25 and 40 million seems a good, if rather broad, guess. Considering our human population of 260 million and all the habitat we've destroyed under suburbs, roadways, plowed fields and shopping malls, today's 25 million deer represent a respectable herd, to say the least. We should guard it jealously.

Chapter One

Origins & Evolution

How Deer Came to Be

Most people overlook some of the more fascinating aspects of whitetails for one simple reason: They can't understand the language. When you read "…ancestral even-toed suborder *Palæodonta* was derived from the *Condylarthra*, an early Tertiary Period assemblage of mammals …" your eyes glaze over and you start looking for a pillow. But cut through the paleontologists' jargon, and you discover that our innocent little whitetail has really "been around the block." A million years ago it was living cheek-to-jowl with mammoths and mastodons, camels, llamas, giant bison and ground sloths the size of African elephants. Imagine that. Our delicate, "modern" looking deer used to hang out with those weird, extinct animals. It also ran from dire wolves and dodged hungry saber-toothed cats. Is it any wonder the whitetail is alert and wary?

Opposite page: It may be hard to believe that this buck's ancestors shared the continent with primitive wolves and saber-toothed tigers. It's no wonder that whitetails are survivors to the utmost degree.

Fossil evidence suggests that whitetails have been around for 6 million years. Humans have been around for only 100,000 years.

But a million years ago is relatively recent history for whitetails. The earliest known whitetail fossil is some 4 million years old. It reportedly matches modern whitetails bone for bone, which means whitetails are living fossils. They probably arose as many as 6 million years ago somewhere near today's U.S.-Canada border. We don't know precisely when or where, because, alas, at least four continental glaciers have since ground their way over that terrain and scoured away most of the fossil evidence. South of this glacial advance, however, fossil hunters have uncovered a rich variety of mammal remains. Would you believe more than 100 extinct mammal species have been identified from the Badlands of South Dakota alone? Those and other fossils from around the world sketch an interesting story of the rise and fall of many strange and wondrous beasts, including some that haven't fallen yet—like whitetails.

Unfortunately, mineralized bones can only hint at the past; they can't provide detailed reports. Paleontologists must study fossil evidence the way detectives study crime scenes. They combine clues from volcanic ash, ancient mud flows, rock strata, continental drift, prehistoric animal scat found in desert caves, even fossilized tree pollen, in order to understand ancient stories of life, death and adaptation. These stories change slightly as new material is unearthed, but the general plot line remains constant: The whitetail evolved as a secretive species hiding in mixed forests where it ate soft plant material—just as it does today.

COMPETING WITH DINO

As most of today's grade school kids know, during the Jurassic period about 200 million years ago, the first mammals scurried in the shadows of dinosaurs. If we saw

LOST GIANTS

Several deer that formerly shared time and space with elk and whitetails are now extinct and that's too bad. Can you imagine stalking an open country deer the size of an elk wearing moose-like antlers 12 feet wide? That's twice the width of a huge Alaska-Yukon moose rack! Such massive antlers were routinely grown by the Irish elk, *Megaceros gigantheus*, whose bony remains are often found in Irish peat bogs. It is presumed to have been a runner much like today's caribou, and it roamed across open grasslands, perhaps tundra, of Europe, Scandinavia and into Siberia. Although it was gone from the British Isles 10,000 years ago, it may have survived as recently as 2,500 years ago in the Black Sea region. Irish farmers have been known to dig up *Megaceros* antlers and lay them across brooks as footbridges—the ultimate in recycling creativity and efficiency.

In North America the stag moose, *Cervalces*, grew three-lobed, palmated antlers and stood as high as today's Alaska-Yukon moose. *Libralces gallicus*, the first moose found in the fossil record, was the size of an elk. Its horns grew out at right angles to its head as extremely long, relatively straight main beams before turning up in palmated ends with numerous points. Its teeth are identical in structure to the dentition of today's moose, so it probably lived in similar moist, brushy habitat.

Other antlered giants emerged and died out in South America and Asia. There is no evidence that primitive man ever hunted them. Rapidly changing climates probably led to the demise of these splendid creatures. Perhaps through advanced cloning, geneticists might someday recreate these lost Pleistocene beasts. What a sight that would be.

one of those ancient mammals today we'd probably set a trap for it and bait it with cheese. The little critters were probably omnivorous, but they essentially lived on dinosaur table scraps because the big monsters hogged most of the foliage. Mammals survived by being inconspicuous.

Against browsing competition from the likes of brontosaurs and triceratops, not to mention predatory attacks from speedy carnivores like velociraptor, a mammal the size of a whitetail wouldn't have stood a chance. Down in the leaves, however, a mouse-sized mammal could squeak by on insects, seeds, leaves and carrion.

At the end of the Cretaceous period about 65 million years ago something went terribly wrong. Worldwide evidence points an accusing finger at a large asteroid that plowed into the Earth off the east coast of Mexico, raising a suffocating cloud of dust that persisted for years. Temperatures dropped, vegetation died and dinosaurs went to their collective Great Reward. The tiny mammals, however, survived in pockets of sedges, grass or perhaps even lichens. It doesn't take much food to keep a wee bit of muscle and bone alive. Oh, some "dinosaurs" hung on, too—primitive birds, crocodiles, sharks, sturgeon, horseshoe crabs and many small lizards, to name a few—but the mega-critters checked out permanently.

About the time whitetails appeared in their current configuration between 4 and 6 million years ago, mankind was still emerging in Africa as *Australopithecus afarensis*, the famous Lucy fossil discovered in Ethiopia. Lucy stood 4 feet tall and walked erect, but her brain was less than one quarter the capacity of *Homo sapiens*. The first fossil evidence of the *Homo* genus, *Homo erectus*, dates back 2 million years.

Modern man didn't arise until sometime between 150,000 and 100,000 years ago and didn't reach North America until 30,000 years ago at the earliest. Since then, humans and whitetails have flourished side by side. As long as we resist the urge to convert all of our forests and fields to subdivisions and highways, that should continue for a long time to come.

BRAVE NEW WORLD

After the dust settled, a cornucopia of new vegetation sprang up, free for the taking. The diminutive mammals responded like a crew of ranch hands turned loose at a smorgasbord. It took them about 15 million years to really pick up speed, but then they quickly (by geologic standards) evolved into hundreds of new species adapted to take advantage of all that unclaimed vegetation. Some remained small and hid in the ground. Some grew long legs and necks to reach treetop leaves. Some climbed trees to reach nuts and buds. Some became semiaquatic to reach cattail roots and pond lilies. Some hopped, some leaped and some, like whitetails, dashed away from danger, then sneaked into hiding. And a few, naturally, took to eating all the new vegetarians.

The *Condylarths*, one of these early mammal groups, were the first to develop some deer-like features. Their molars were rather broad and rounded instead of pointed, indicating a mostly plant diet. And instead of walking on their soles like raccoons and humans (plantigrade), *Condylarths* developed hoof-like nails (ungules, from which the term ungulate comes) and began walking on their toes (digitigrade). Paleontologists have identified 90 extinct genera of these "pre-ungulate"

Opposite page: Whitetailed deer thrive in diverse habitats, from northern conifer forests to southern swamps to Arizona deserts and even here at snowcovered Devil's Tower in Wyoming.

This Alberta buck succumbed to the rigors of winter. Fortunately, enough of his brethren will survive—as they have for millenia—to perpetuate the species.

beasts. Some grew as large as modern bears. None survive today, but their descendants, highly modified, do.

BRANCHING OUT

From their early beginnings mammals branched into a number of orders, many of which died out completely (*Titanotheres, Dinocerata*), a few of which still hang on today (elephants, manatees), and some which flowered to become what are now the most successful mid- to large-sized herbivores on Earth. These are the odd-toed *Perissodactyls* (horses, tapirs and rhinos) and the even-toed *Artiodactyls* (sheep, pigs, camels, giraffes, antelope, cattle and—aha!—deer).

The earliest known horse was the famous *Eohippus* with four-toed front feet and three-toed hind feet. Over eons *Eohippus* evolved into the three-toed *Miohippus* and eventually the one-toed horse we know today. The deer-family equivalent of *Eohippus* is a rabbit-sized creature called *Diacodexis*, the first fossil mammal that sported two-hoofed toes perched at the end of a lengthened ankle bone. This creature's teeth were shaped for mashing relatively tender herbs and leaves. Believe it or not, the *Diacodexis* fossil is between 58 and 63 million years old. It had no antlers; they would come later.

Compared to antlers, feet and toes are boring appendages, but they are much more critical to an animal's survival. Deer can live without antlers, as millions of females prove each year, but they can't live without feet. The development of the long "ankle" or metatarsal bones in deer increased their leverage, enabling them to stay one jump ahead of their predators. All this fancy footwork partly explains why deer-like mammals prospered while heavily-built, lumbering beasts like the snout-horned *Brontothere*, larger than today's rhino, faded away.

Diacodexis not only survived but spawned a variety of similar two-toed herbivores throughout the Eocene epoch roughly 58 million to 36 million years ago. At first these primitive ungulates (hoofed herbivores) were small creatures living in forests and forest edges where competition for a limited food supply was stiff. We guess this was the case because their fossilized skeletons closely resemble today's most primitive deer, the antlerless but fanged—that's right, fanged—musk deer of China. Some scientists don't even consider the musk deer a true deer, but it's obviously a close relative. Musk deer sneak about in heavy foliage alone or in mated pairs, marking their territories with droppings and scent glands and defending them (thus the fangs) from others of their species. That's probably how our whitetail's early ancestors behaved.

The fossil bones from a number of Eocene "proto-deer" show a progression from fangs to antlers. *Blastomeryx* had fangs but no head gear. *Aletomeryx* had fangs too, but it also sported knob-like bones atop its little head. Hmmm. *Cranioceras* had no fangs and even longer protruding head bones. Now we're getting somewhere. *Lagomeryx* sported forked bones several inches long. None of these bones were shed like true antlers. Apparently they were permanent, skin-covered protuberances similar to giraffe horns—or perhaps like a modern whitetail's velvet antlers.

BROWSERS & GRAZERS

Taxonomists are scientists who organize and file life forms like a good secretary files office papers: a place for everything and everything in its place. They study anatomy, grouping insects with insects, spiders with arachnids and whales with mammals instead of fish. As defining characteristics narrow, classes of animals become orders, then suborders, then infraorders, families, genera, species and, finally, subspecies. The deeper into the filing system you pry, the narrower and more specific the anatomical distinctions.

Even though deer, cattle and sheep all fall within the *Artiodactyla* order, the *Ruminantia* suborder and the *Pecora* infraorder, something significant separates them after that level: their teeth. Whitetails and other deer have low-crowned molars designed to mash relatively soft plant tissue, that of herbs, tree leaves and shrubbery. Bison and sheep have high-crowned molars, which enable them to masticate the tougher, silca-rich grasses. This difference explains why bison and sheep live largely in open grasslands while whitetails stick mainly to woods and brush. There are substantial differences in stomach and intestine structures between browsers and grazers, too, which is covered in the anatomy section of this book (see pages 74–81).

THE FIRST DEER

Finally there is *Dicrocerus*, the first known antler-bearing mammal. It lived some 36 million years ago in what today is Europe. This primitive deer probably weighed about 30 pounds, the size of today's muntjacs, a subfamily of Asian deer with short, primitive spike antlers and short canine fangs. Enlarged canine teeth or fangs appear in several living deer, including elk, whose "ivories" or whistle teeth are highly prized trophies of the hunt. Occasionally a whitetail will be found with small upper canines, a genetic throwback to an ancient heritage.

It would be nice if there were a steady progression of fossils illustrating further

Right: Unlike their mule deer relatives, whitetails are rarely encountered far from water. In the West, you usually see whitetails along the riverbottoms, whereas mulies are more commonly found higher up on the slopes. Opposite page: This buck probably looks a lot like his ancestors did 4 million years ago.

development of the deer family (*Cervidae*), but the next fossils appearing in the line are full-blown "modern" deer such as elk, moose, caribou and whitetails.

There is evidence that the subfamily *Cervinae*, which includes elk, red deer, fallow deer and several other Asian species, arose in Eurasia and is probably older than the *Odocoileinae* subfamily, which evolved in North America. The American line includes our whitetails plus mule deer, blacktails, all South American deer, one Chinese water deer, the Eurasian roe deer, moose and caribou. Obviously these species didn't all develop from the whitetail. Rather, most evolved off a common ancestral stock back when North America was still connected to Europe. Many biologists do believe, however, that when the isthmus of Central America finally connected the two American continents, whitetails drifted south and gave rise to all South American deer. These include the world's smallest deer, the 12-pound, spike-antlered Pudu of the northern Andes mountains.

The big question is how did European deer such as the elk end up dodging cowboys in Montana while American deer like the caribou and moose find themselves ducking Sven and Ole in Sweden? The answer, of course, is that Europe and North America were connected before the continents drifted apart. And at various times North America and Siberia were connected via the famous Bering Sea "land bridge" between Alaska and Siberia. When more of the Earth's water was tied up in glaciers, sea levels were hundreds of feet lower than they are today. So, while elk were trekking east toward Fairbanks, they might have passed moose and caribou walking west toward Moscow. Our little whitetail, however, seemed content to

stay home, virtually unchanged for at least 4 million years, perfectly adapted to life in the mixed brushland, forests and meadows of North America where we still find it today: a living fossil thriving at the dawn of the 21st century.

FORGED BY COMPETITION

Predators like this coyote have helped mold whitetails into the survival machines they are. This coyote chased a button buck onto the ice, where the deer became easy prey.

Whitetails didn't just accidentally become the tough, adaptable survivors they are today. They were molded by their environment, including vegetation, climate, competing herbivores and various predators. Because whitetails sprang from deer-like animals that lived within the protection of forests and shrub lands, they evolved teeth and digestive systems to maximize exploitation of such foliage. Because bear, dog, and cat-like predators skulked through those woods, whitetails evolved a four-chambered stomach which they could fill quickly, thus minimizing their exposure in the open. Afterwards they could retreat into cover to re-chew and digest this food safely. Whitetails also developed sensitive noses and ears to detect predators, silent behaviors and dull pelage to hide from them, and a fast, explosive run to escape them. Whitetail fawns, too weak and slow to outrun predators, are odorless, motionless and camouflaged by spotted coats.

To compete successfully against the giant plant browsers of the day, such as 10-foot ground sloths and various primitive elephants, whitetails remained small, quick and adaptable so they could exploit low, new plant growth that sprouted after over-browsing, fires and floods. Instead of subsisting on a handful of plant species, they learned to eat a wide range of plants, fruits and seeds. They lived alone or in small herds to minimize their impact on vegetation and survive where larger critters might have starved. When grasslands increased, whitetails wisely stuck to their brush and woods to avoid competing against dozens of new grazing species like horses, sheep, elk, bison and camels.

As climates became colder, whitetails evolved dense winter coats that trapped dead air for insulation, then shed the heavy coats for thin, uninsulated summer coats. The survivors piled on body fat to see them through lean times and shifted their metabolism so that they required less forage during winter. They began to communicate through scents rather than sounds or sights, so as to keep track of one

Young fawns are nearly odorless, and it's rare to see them up and moving around until they gain enough strength to outrun predators.

PLEISTOCENE EXTINCTION: THE GREAT MYSTERY

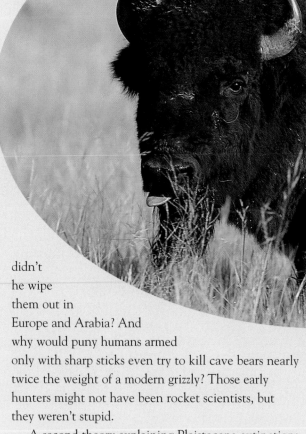

Animals have been going extinct on Earth for millions of years. Some 90 percent of all identified species live no more. Typically a generic line of animals will evolve new species better adapted to changing habitat conditions before old species die out. The long line of extinct, primitive horses is a prime example.

Only twice have species abruptly passed away in waves without leaving evolutionary replacements. The first mass extinction was the big dinosaur die-off, which most scientists credit to an asteroid. The second was the great Pleistocene mammal extinction from 15,000 to about 9,000 years ago. There is no extraterrestrial evidence for this mass killing. Worldwide, some 200 genera slipped away, most of them large mammals: what we would term big-game animals. Of about 70 species lost in North America, only three were small mammals. Just three of 69 known reptile and amphibian species were wiped out. Clearly, something was selecting big mammals. Could it have been our ancestors?

The massive die-off coincided with man's appearance on this continent, leading some paleontologists to blame human over-hunting for the disaster. Indeed, worldwide Pleistocene extinction closely follows mankind's spread across the globe from Africa to Australia. Prior to man's arrival, few large mammals made their final exit. Clovis flint spear points have been found with mammoth bones. Folsom points and even reindeer-antler spear points have been found stuck in the mineralized bones of giant bison.

Many modern hunters find it hard to believe that their Stone Age predecessors could have completely wiped out so many large mammals. If 18th-century Paleo-Indians armed with horses and bows didn't exterminate modern bison, how could isolated tribes of unmounted men with stone-tipped spears destroy the giant bison, a once-common species nearly twice the size of today's bison? If man killed off mammoths in Europe, Siberia and North America, why didn't he eliminate elephants from Africa and India? If he killed all the horses and camels in North America, why

didn't he wipe them out in Europe and Arabia? And why would puny humans armed only with sharp sticks even try to kill cave bears nearly twice the weight of a modern grizzly? Those early hunters might not have been rocket scientists, but they weren't stupid.

A second theory explaining Pleistocene extinctions holds that post-glacial dessication (the climate dried out) doomed the grassland herbivores across the Great Plains and Southwest. Horses, giant bison, four-horned pronghorns, giant sloths, mammoths and camels died for lack of forage while woodland species like moose, elk and whitetails survived in the wetter East. But this doesn't account for the survival of today's bison and pronghorn, nor does it explain why the giant beaver died out while the modern beaver survived.

Diseases migrating across the Bering Land Bridge with man, elk, sheep and other Eurasian species is another proposal. But few bacteria or viruses completely destroy their host species. Not even the bubonic plague—the Black Death—could kill every European. There are always immune individuals who survive and pass on their immunity to future generations.

Some paleobiologists suggest that changing climate during the Ice Age may have doomed the young of large species with long gestation periods. If spring were delayed by just a month or two, young herbivores might have starved. But with this scenario, wouldn't more southerly living individuals of each species have survived? Could climates have changed so abruptly, harshly and extensively that species died before they could migrate to more favorable climates? And again, why would giant bison die but not modern bison?

Probably a combination of changing habitats, changing weather, disease and predation killed off all those Pleistocene beasts. But only the survivors know for sure, and they aren't talking.

What we do know is that the great Pleistocene extinction denied us the joy of sharing our forests and grasslands with an amazing variety of wonderful animals that would add spice to our outdoor adventures. Just some of the species gone forever are: Smilodon, a saber-toothed cat the size of an African lion; Eremotherium, a ground sloth as tall as a giraffe; Tremarctotheres, a short-faced bear the size of a Kodiak brown bear; mammoths and mastodons, genuine North American elephants; Camelops, a camel whose mummified remains have been found in caves in Utah; Capromeryx, a jackrabbit-sized pronghorn; Stockoceros, a four-horned pronghorn; Bootherium, a woodland muskox.

Whatever killed this incredibly varied and fascinating bestiary couldn't wipe out our tough little whitetail, still the king of deer.

An old survivor: A mature buck with a blind eye and bare throat patch, most likely the result of rutting battles.

Whitetails are adaptable and opportunistic feeders, shifting their food focus with the habitat and the seasons. This buck diligently searches through the leaves for dropped acorns.

another without alerting voracious neighbors. Cycles adjusted so does could give birth when spring plant production was peaking for maximum nutrition. By dropping all their fawns within a short time frame they overwhelmed predators: some fawns always survived. While cats and dogs were digesting the first few fawns they caught, the others were growing stronger, faster and more difficult to catch.

Like many of Earth's most successful species, whitetails have thrived for millions of years because they are adaptable. That's always a good strategy on a planet where change is the only constant. If fire burns down your oak forest, eat the raspberry vines that spring up. If a flood washes away the cottonwoods, move into the willow thicket. If the tasty upland forbs grow where there is no cover, spend the day in a bordering cattail jungle, slipping out at dusk and dawn to fill up.

Thanks to the harsh environment in which they evolved, whitetails are like the country boys glorified in verse and song: When times get tough, they have the skill and will to survive.

THE WORLD'S LIVING DEER

Even though too many mammals were lost during the Pleistocene, quite a few deer still survive. In order to better understand our whitetail, it's important to know a bit about its distant cousins. Depending on whom you believe, there are anywhere from 30 to 70 species of deer left in the world. This huge discrepancy is due, of course, to lumping and splitting. For instance, because red deer, Siberian elk, North American elk and Japanese sika deer can be crossbred to produce fertile offspring, lumpers like to call them all variations of the red deer. But splitters compare an 800-pound Yellowstone elk to a 120-pound sika buck and shake their heads. These are obviously different species. The rest of us can just relax and enjoy all our remaining varieties of deer, regardless of how closely or distantly they're related.

LIVING MEMBERS OF THE DEER FAMILY

Musk Deer (3 species): Some people believe that these primitive Asian deer should constitute a distinct family of their own. They have no antlers, but males have 4-inch tusks for fighting other males. Does have only two mammary glands compared to four in all other deer. Males average 23 pounds; females 28 pounds. Musk deer stand about 20 inches high at shoulder and are hump-backed. They live in dense forests, and males sport a single musk gland on their bellies. These deer are widely pursued for musk used in the perfume industry.

- Siberian musk deer (*Moschus moschiferus*)
- Dwarf musk deer (*Moschus Berezovski*)
- Alpine musk deer (*Moschus chrysogaster*)

Water Deer (1 species): This is the Chinese water deer (*Hydropotes inermis*), similar to musk deer. Males average 24 pounds; females slightly less, and they stand 20 inches at the shoulder. They have no antlers. The male sports canines 2 to 3 inches long. These deer prefer lowland grass and marsh near rivers in China and Korea.

Muntjacs (5 species plus related tufted deer): This odd Asiatic woodland and forest deer has unusually long pedicles starting at the eyebrow and reaching back to create twin ridges on the skull. External antlers are but short spikes no more than 7 inches long, often with brow tines. Males grow 1- to 2-inch-long tusks. They are small deer, ranging from

Male muntjac.

24 to 40 pounds and standing 16 to 25 inches at the shoulder. Males bark. These deer breed year-round, regardless of the male's stage of antler growth.

- Indian muntjac (*Muntiacus muntjac*) 15 subspecies
- Reeves or Chinese muntjac (*M. reevesi*) 2 subspecies
- Black muntjac (*M. crinifrons*)
- Fea's muntjac (*M. feae*)
- Roosevelt's muntjac (*M. rooseveltorum*)
- Tufted deer (*Elaphodus cephalophus*) 3 subspecies

EURASIAN DEER

This large subfamily, *Cervinae*, includes many large and popular big-game species, including our own wapiti or North American elk. Included are four genera with 14 species and roughly 75 subspecies! Let's get started.

Red deer (*Cervus elephus*): A dozen subspecies of this widespread deer live from the British Isles to north Africa, Scandinavia, Tibet and Afghanistan; they have also been introduced in Argentina, Australia and New Zealand. Red deer have blunted ivories (canines) like North American elk and roar instead of bugle. Antler conformation is similar to an elk's, but has more crowning points at the end. Size varies widely by subspecies, from about 250 to 660 pounds. They have adapted to various habitats from woodlands to grasslands.

Sika deer (*C. nippon*): 13 subspecies. This small cousin of the red deer stands about 32 inches at the shoulder and weighs about 120 pounds. Its summer coat is unusual in that it is flecked with white spots. Antlers are shaped similar to an elk's, but are small with four or five points. Sika deer are native to the Japanese islands, southeast China, Vietnam and Manchuria.

Sika deer.

Wapiti (*C. canadensis*): This is another name for the common elk of North America. It's recognized as the same species found in east China, Mongolia and Manchuria, and it has been introduced in New Zealand. Weight varies from 500 to nearly 1,000 pounds. As many as 13 subspecies have been cataloged at one time or another.

Sambar (*C. unicolor*): 16 subspecies. This is India's version of the red deer. It stands from 2 feet to nearly 4½ feet tall and weighs up to 600 pounds. The antlers are shaped like an elk's, but with just three points. Sambar near the equator often keep one rack for several years before casting it.

Rusa deer or **Javan deer** (*C. timorensis*): 6 or 7 subspecies on Indonesian islands. Once considered a subspecies of Sambar, this deer has similar antlers and a slightly smaller body. Antler cycles are irregular.

Barasingha or **swamp deer** (*C. duvauceli*): 2 subspecies, India and Nepal, both swamp dwellers. Native to the base of Himalayas, these deer are now endangered. Their tall racks look like a multi-tined cross between mule deer and whitetail.

Eld's deer, thamin or **brow-antlered deer** (*C. eldi*): 3 subspecies, all rare now. This unusual marsh deer of Thailand and Burma walks flat-footed on its pasterns, rather than on its hoof tips like most deer, to afford better footing in its marsh habitat. It is roughly the size of average whitetail, but antlers may reach 3 feet in length.

Thorold's deer (*C. albirostris*): This deer weighs about 300 pounds, with hooves short and wide like those of cattle. Hair grows backward on its withers, giving the appearance of a hump. These deer live in high-altitude rhododendron forests and grasslands in eastern Tibet and China.

Pere David's deer (*Elaphurus davidiensis*): This rare deer was never known in the wild. Discovered in 1865 by French missionary Armand David south of Peking in an imperial hunting park, private and zoo herds are now maintained in several countries. Reintroductions have been tried in China. This deer stands just over 4 feet at the shoulder and weighs 440 pounds. The antlers are unique in that tines project backward from tall main beams (like elk antlers in reverse). Another oddity: The antlers are in velvet during winter, stripping in May or June. The deer ruts in summer, carrying the calves 9 months for birth in April or May. Hooves are splayed wide as if adapted to marshy ground.

Fallow deer (*Dama dama*): 2 subspecies in Europe and Iran. Widely introduced around the world, this popular game species exists on many Texas ranches. Fallow deer are about whitetail size with spotted or

Pere David's deer.

Right: Fallow deer.
Below: Roe deer.

all-white coats. Antlers are tall like an elk's but palmated like that of a moose. Wild populations no longer exist.

Chital or spotted deer (*Axis axis*): 2 subspecies. Another spotted deer, possibly closely related to similar-sized fallow deer. Antlers are tall but not palmated. This is the common Indian deer that tigers love to eat. Wild populations have been introduced in Hawaii and it is sometimes managed on Texas game ranches.

Hog deer (*A. porcinus*): 2 subspecies. Named for its heavy build, the hog deer stands about 28 inches at the shoulder and weighs about 90 pounds. They live in dense grass which they rush through like pigs rather than bound over like deer. Native to India and Vietnam, hog deer have an irregular antler and breeding cycle typical of tropical deer.

Bawean or **Kuhl's deer** (*A. kuhli*): Similar to hog deer but restricted to a single island between Java and Borneo. It is very rare.

Calamian deer (*A. calamianensis*): Another rare island version of the hog deer, restricted to the Calamian islands of the Philippines.

NEW WORLD DEER

Finally, we find our whitetail in the subfamily *Odocoileinae*, along with mule deer, moose and similar familiar species. The only European representative is the common roe deer. These are some of the most evolved deer in the world.

Roe deer (*Capreolus capreolus*): 3 subspecies scattered from Europe to China and Korea, north to Siberia. This deer is an adaptable colonizer like the whitetail but much smaller. The European version stands 28 inches at shoulder and weighs only 50 pounds. Siberian subspecies are twice as big. Antlers are 5- to 8-inch spikes with one or two tines. Some think this species may have given rise to our whitetail back when Europe and North America were still connected.

White-tailed deer (*Odocoileus virginianus*): Here's our local hero, represented by 17 to 38 subspecies—depending on how you group them—from central Canada to central South America.

Above: Whitetail.
Below: Mule deer.

Mule deer (*O. hemionus*): Research indicates the mule deer was created relatively recently by the direct mating of male Columbia black-tailed deer with female whitetails; so this is our newest species. Blacktails arose earlier from whitetail stem stock, then became isolated on the Pacific coast where they underwent gradual changes in response to their unique wet forest environment.

Red brocket (*Mazama americana*): 14 jungle-dwelling subspecies from Mexico through Central America to Argentina. Brockets can reach up to 45 pounds with short spike antlers. They live in dense jungle thickets and eat an almost exclusive fruit diet.

Brown brocket (M. *gouazoubira*): 10 subspecies. Similar size and distribution to the red brocket but lives in more open woodland habitats.

Little red brocket (M. *rufina*): 2 subspecies in forest thickets from Venezuela, Ecuador and southeast Brazil. Another fruit eater.

Dwarf brocket (M. *chunyi*): Scientists didn't discover this little deer until the mid-1940s. Little is known about this resident of Northern Bolivia and Peru.

Southern pudu (*Pudu puda*): This deer stands just 15 inches at the shoulder and weighs up to only 22 pounds. This is a dark forest dweller in the lower Andes of Chile and Argentina. It sports tiny spikes.

Northern pudu (*P. mephistopheles*): 2 subspecies. This deer is like the southern pudu but lives in the Andes of northern Peru, Ecuador and Colombia.

Marsh deer (*Blastocerus dichotomus*): The marsh deer lives in Argentina and Brazil in open-country grasslands near rivers. This is the largest South American deer, about the size of a good Dakota whitetail. Rare and declining.

Pampas deer (*Ozotocerus bezoarticus*): 3 subspecies inhabit Brazil, Argentina, Paraguay and Bolivia. Small, straight antlers with up to 3 tines like those of the roe deer. A strong, disagreeable odor reportedly carries to the meat. The species is still near extinction due to habitat destruction and exploitation. It is an open-country animal.

Chilean huemul (*Hippocamelus bisulcus*): A high country, grassland and brush deer living up to nosebleed altitudes in the Andes of Chile and western Argentina. This is the southernmost deer in the world. It stands 3 feet at the shoulder and is solidly built. The antlers fork right at the base, giving the impression of four antlers. It sports large, mule-like ears.

Peruvian huemel or **taruca** (*H. antisensis*): This deer of Peru, Ecuador, Bolivia and northern Argentina closely resembles the Chilean huemul.

Moose (*Alces alces*): 6 subspecies. This well-known character needs little introduction. It is the world's largest living deer, growing to up to 1,400 pounds and 6½ feet tall at the shoulders. This American species has expanded west to Scandinavia.

Caribou/Reindeer (*Rangifer trandus*): 9 subspecies. This is the world's most northern deer, Santa's helper. Caribou have the largest antler-to-body weight ratio of all deer. They stand 4 feet at the shoulder and weigh up to 550 pounds. Reindeer are so named because they've been trained to pull sleds by Laplanders who control them with reins.

WHITETAIL SUBSPECIES

Hunters and taxonomists alike have argued over whitetail classifications for years and aren't about to stop now. Splitters see the slightest differences between deer from region to region and immediately designate them subspecies: They've named roughly 30 in North and Central America. In the U.S. and Canada, splitters generally agree on 13 subspecies, plus four more isolated on South Carolina coastal islands. Lumpers disregard small anatomical differences and throw most whitetails into a big melting pot. After all, they'll all interbreed and produce fertile young.

Everyone can agree that there is a major difference between a 300-pound Dakota whitetail buck and a 75-pound Key deer buck, but how do we know where the Texas subspecies stops and the Kansas subspecies starts? According to the taxonomists' maps, Texas deer range halfway up western Kansas and eastern Colorado, yet old Plains bucks in the vicinity of Lamar and Dodge City commonly weigh 240 to 300 pounds, while mature bucks southwest of San Antonio are lucky to reach 200 pounds.

Top: Florida Key buck.
Above: Dakota whitetail.

The diminutive Coues' whitetail of the Southwest desert mountains is an isolated and obvious subspecies, but where do we draw the line between the boreal northwoods whitetail of Minnesota and the Dakota whitetail?

Nitpickers cite things like cranial details, external dimensions, pelt color and antler-tine size to distinguish among regional variations, but this gets difficult as deer mingle along subspecies boundaries. And over the years various transplant programs designed to reestablish

herds, impart hybrid vigor or increase antler size have muddied the blood lines. Boreal deer have been introduced in the South and Texas; Virginia whitetails have been shipped north. Dakota deer have moved east. It seems that most whitetails are part of the great American melting pot by now.

Obviously, splitting the species up isn't precise. We can see that geographic averages sharply defined near the center of the subspecies' range get fuzzy out on the edges. This reflects the gradual shift in habitat, climate, vegetation and other factors that influence whitetail physiology. Simply put, the longer a deer has evolved under local influences, the more it will resemble a distinct subspecies. A Kansas whitetail will look unmistakably like a Kansas whitetail on the outskirts of Salina. But it will look more like a Virginia whitetail along the Mississippi near St. Louis, more like a Texas whitetail just west of Dallas, and more like a Dakota whitetail near Omaha. Until you get to extremes in habitat—like the Florida Keys or the Arizona desert mountains— differences are subtle. Leave them to the experts to decipher.

What the average hunter will notice about whitetails' physical appearances follows some universal rules of biology.

Bergmann's Rule states that body mass increases with distance from the equator. Thus, the farther north you go, the taller, longer and wider whitetails tend to be. This makes them more efficient in the cold since a large body mass retains core heat better than a small body mass does. The bigger beast has more internal volume per unit of surface. Anyone who's shot both a Dakota buck and a Coues' buck knows the truth of Bergmann's Rule. You'll bust your belly dragging a

Dakota out; you can practically sling a Coues' over your shoulder and skip home.

Allen's Rule is a corollary to Bergmann's. It states that the farther warm-blooded animals live from the equator, the shorter grow their extremities. Why? So they don't freeze off! Well, more precisely so they don't radiate too much heat and waste it. Conversely, deer in hot climates need large extremities, to expose more surface to the air and get rid of excess body heat. Once again, the Coues' deer/Dakota deer comparison bears this out. Northcountry whitetails have the smallest ears and tails; Coues' deer have the largest ears and tails.

Antlers don't fall under Allen's Rule because, while they do radiate body heat during their velvet stage, they do not during their hardened stage. Besides, they fall off in winter, and this is the brutal season that most influences extremity size. However, we could make up a new rule—call it **Spomer's Antler Rule**—stating that antler size in white-tailed deer increases with body size. Sure enough, Key and Coues' deer grow the smallest antlers of all North American subspecies; Dakota and boreal bucks

Boreal whitetail in velvet.

grow the largest. The number-one typical whitetail of all time is the Dakota subspecies Hanson Buck from Saskatchewan. The number two is the boreal subspecies Jordan Buck from Wisconsin. Number three is a boreal from Illinois. Number four is a Dakota from Alberta.

Gloger's Rule holds that mammals in warm, humid habitats have darker pelage than their kin in open, dry habitats. This is basic camouflage at work. In sunny habitats with pale soils and vegetation, light pelts blend in better than do dark pelts. In shadowy woods, dark hides do the job. One wonders, though, how much of this apparent tonal difference is genetic and how much a result of simple solar bleaching. Out on the Plains, at least, whitetail pelts fade to an ever-whiter shade of pale as winter drags on. By May those ragged old coats are bleached nearly white by the sun!

Top: *Texas whitetail.*
Above: *Young Northwest whitetail.*

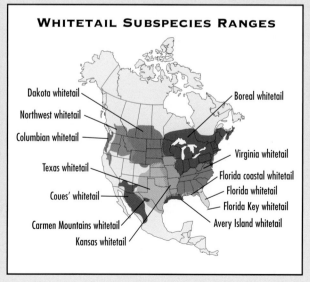

WHITETAIL SUBSPECIES RANGES

Dakota whitetail
Northwest whitetail
Columbian whitetail
Texas whitetail
Coues' whitetail
Carmen Mountains whitetail
Kansas whitetail
Boreal whitetail
Virginia whitetail
Florida coastal whitetail
Florida whitetail
Florida Key whitetail
Avery Island whitetail

CHAPTER TWO
ANATOMY

PREDATOR DEFENSES

ENGINEERED TO RUN & HIDE

Perspective is an interesting phenomenon. It seemingly changes reality. Drastically. For instance, if you are a sensitive urbanite recently converted to vegetarianism, a whitetail is a delicate flame of innocent life burning bright against the cruel injustice of man's brave new world. But if you are a kernel of corn, ripe with the promise of new life and charged with the genetic responsibility to create the next generation of your kind, a whitetail is a heartless monster, a cruel and insensitive predator out to kill you and thousands more kernels like you. Crunch, crunch—and your life is over.

If, however, you are a coyote with a den of helpless puppies to feed, a whitetail is salvation, dinner on the hoof, animated protein miraculously provided for your dining pleasure. Rip, tear, and your family is saved.

Nature designed deer to eat and be eaten. A long list of predators depends on the whitetail for sustenance, including this bobcat (opposite). But whitetails have effective defenses against their predators.

53

Ever on the alert! Does tend to travel in matriarchal groups of related individuals, providing more eyes to watch out for danger.

As for the whitetail itself, well, it thinks it is the center of the universe. We can guess this by its selfish behavior. It does not gather up food for other species. It doesn't forego gobbling even a single acorn so that a hungry squirrel might have it instead. No, a whitetail lives only for itself, only for today. A doe is so selfish that she will strike out at her own fawn to drive it from a bough of tasty balsam needles in a wintering yard. From a whitetail's point of view, the great, green world of vegetation was created solely as its private smorgasbord.

JUST ANOTHER BRICK IN THE WALL

Nature has a slightly different perspective altogether. She sees the whitetail as just another cog in the wheel of life, no more or less important than the self-appointed vegetarian, the innocent kernel of corn or the predacious coyote. Specifically, nature sees the whitetail as a converter, a hairy chemical-manufacturing plant designed to take in vegetation and turn it into a substance—meat—that other life forms can use to power their own engines. Nature designed whitetails to eat and be eaten.

Despite this reality, there probably isn't an adult alive in America who hasn't at some time heard or uttered this sentiment about deer: *How can anyone kill such a beautiful animal?* Ouch. How do you defend against that? Are you really so insensitive, heartless and aesthetically perverse as to want to destroy natural beauty? The very idea sounds monstrous. Yet the real question should be: *How can you not want to kill such a beautiful animal?* Just as rose petals attract bees, whitetails attract predators. They look good, they smell good and they taste good. Virtually every creature with the slightest carnivorous leanings wants to sink its teeth into whitetails:

cougars, jaguars, wolves, black bears, coyotes, bobcats, alligators, even giant snakes down in the tropics. And, of course, us. For at least 10,000 years, whitetails have been adapting to human predation. This is a good thing: Without predators constantly pressing and challenging them, whitetails would not be the soft-eyed, graceful beauties they are.

PRETTY FOR A REASON

Think about what makes a whitetail attractive. Long legs with which it leaps and bounds gracefully, almost effortlessly over logs and waterways. Large, liquid eyes for detecting the slightest motion in dim light. Big ears that swivel like radar to catch the merest whisper of a rustle. A long, sensitive nose that guides the rest of the body through a potential minefield of suspicious odors. A long, graceful neck to raise all these defensive weapons above the brush and project them around trunks without exposing the vulnerable body to attack. Spots to conceal helpless fawns in dappled light, bark-brown pelage for wintering adults, and that bright, flashing tail for alerting other deer to trouble afoot. All these wonderful design features are tied to an alert, ever-watchful demeanor and sharp, quick escape responses.

Truly, predatory attacks over millions of years have molded the whitetail into

You can see that the ears on this buck are swiveling independently of one another to catch sounds. Even in the rut (note the swollen neck), he's a survivor.

quite a fetching package. Without this constant threat of capture, our favorite deer would look less attractive. With nothing chasing them, whitetails wouldn't need their strong, long, graceful legs. They could slither toward their food. With no need to watch for sneaking cougars, they wouldn't need those big, beautiful eyes. Those big, sensitive, rotating ears? Superfluous when nothing ever tries creeping up on you. The long, graceful neck would be senseless. Fawns wouldn't need attractive spots for hiding in the dappled forest since nothing would be looking for them. And that flashing white tail? Of course not. Why signal an alarm if your mates can barely see and no evil predators are after you anyway? So there you have it. A perfectly safe, perfectly content and perfectly ugly white-tailed deer designed by compassion. What a picture of natural loveliness.

Fortunately, Nature is more practical than compassionate. We might not always like Nature's plan, but so far it has worked pretty well. Whitetails have survived in their current form for at least 4 million years and show no signs of giving up. Let's take a closer look at how they flourish in the face of constant predatory pressure.

HIDER EXTRAORDINAIRE

The average observer might think a whitetail's first line of defense is flight. Actually that's nearly its last, just ahead of standing to fight with flailing hoofs and sometimes lowered antlers. What our favorite deer mostly depends on to protect itself from attackers is its habitat. Remember, this animal evolved as a hider species in dense vegetation and remains so to this day, taking advantage of dense brush, reeds, grass and second-growth forests to obstruct and evade prying eyes. Wolves and coyotes might spot pronghorns on the grasslands from a thousand yards, yet fail to see white-tails mere feet away. So long as the wind blows from predator to deer, a whitetail can lie still in heavy cover and avoid detection. This is why wise old bucks often lie like

Left: A Wyoming buck in a pine forest takes advantage of the dense vegetation to obstruct prying eyes. Whitetails don't run unless they have to!
Opposite page: You're done for: This big buck has you pegged.

logs until you nearly step on them. And even then they might not move at all, they've learned through instinct and experience that he who jumps last lasts longer.

Pheasant hunters sometimes flush whitetails from isolated patches of cover in farm fields. The deer, thinking they are safe inside their little hideaway of dense vegetation, stand their ground until the last second. Then the young does and fawns break out, shocking everyone. After heartbeats slow, the hunters resume their march only to flush a young buck. Once its tail has disappeared into a distant woodlot, the shaken bird hunters straighten their caps and again step forward. This is usually when the biggest, baddest buck they've ever seen leaps from its hiding place at their feet (if he even moves at all), a dramatic example of natural selection and learned behavior at work. Young deer that panic at the panting of an approaching coyote draw attention to themselves and are likely to be chased down and devoured. Those that sit tight live to sit another day. The experienced buck or doe that has conquered its nerves a time or two learns to trust its natural ability to blend into its environment, which brings us to whitetail defense number two.

CAMOUFLAGE

The whitetail's second defense—a camouflage coat—is essential to the success of its first. This pelage is neither elaborate nor tricky. Just an average, uniformly dull brown or gray in winter, a brighter reddish brown in summer. Yet, in a remarkable variety of habitats from green summer brush to gray autumn rocks to snowy winter branches, whitetails blend with their environment. On a cloudy day in late autumn woods a whitetail's coat so nearly matches the hues of deciduous trees that human hunters overlook dozens more deer than they ever see. Bobcats and coyotes, being

Even while the does are more active, bucks stay bedded for most of the day.

nearly colorblind, probably miss even more. They detect motion much more readily than they detect color or form, which explains why whitetails have developed their third defense.

SLOW & STEADY WINS THE RACE

Defense number three is attitude: a controlled, patient, confident attitude. It works in conjunction with camouflage and cover to empower a buck, doe or fawn to lie still when the coast is not clear—when the sights, scents and sounds of potential destruction draw near. Ideally a deer wants to detect predators from afar and sneak away undetected, but often this isn't possible. That's when it pays to be calm. Many bowhunters have quietly climbed into their stands and sat for an hour or more before finally noticing a deer bedded nearby. Perhaps the flick of an ear finally gave it away. As the hunter watches, he realizes how calmly a whitetail rests. Hour after

Young deer learn about all aspects of life—and evading predators— from adults.

hour an old deer will lie quietly chewing cud, barely flicking its ears to ward off flies. These movements could be dismissed by predators as birds or butterflies. The older the deer, the less it moves. An old buck might bed at 7 a.m. and not arise until noon, when he'll simply stand, stretch, urinate, turn around and lie down again until dark.

In contrast, half-grown fawns will stand to watch a squirrel or to check out the snap of a twig. They'll walk about, nip vegetation or frolic with young compatriots. Yearlings play less, but still arise more often than older deer to relieve themselves, grab a bite to eat, move to a more comfortable bed. Often does and their fawns will

ODOR AIDERS

Atmospheric conditions can hinder or aid deer in their scenting abilities. Ideal conditions are humidity between 60 and 70 percent, moderate to warm temperatures and light, variable breezes. Heavy mists, drizzle and rain seem to overwhelm scent molecules, often washing them to the ground. Extremely dry air seems to burn them up, or at least make them barely detectable a short distance from their source. Moisture-less air also dries out nasal passages, making them less sensitive. Quiet, humid air with slightly dropping temperatures carries odors down from their source and outward in a cone shape. Warm, dry air carries molecules up where they dissipate quickly. Extreme cold reduces volatility and humidity. Since cold air sinks, most scent flows near the surface. Steady breezes up to 20 mph carry solid, dependable olfactory messages. Bigger winds mix and tear odors, confusing deer.

get up at midday to browse for an hour or two, perhaps move a few hundred yards, but generally they, too, keep motion to a minimum.

Even when traveling, old deer are slow and cautious. During its 2- to 4-mph saunter toward an evening feed field, a buck might stop at the slightest scent or sound and stare for five, 10, even 15 minutes. It might hesitate, motionless, just inside dense cover at the edge of the field, watching, listening, sniffing. Whitetails are like bush plane pilots: There are no old, bold ones. The survivors are calm and cautious. At the same time they're as alert as Olympic sprinters at the starting line, ready to leap away in an instant.

THE NOSE KNOWS

Regardless of how craftily a whitetail hides, eventually a predator finds it. This is why the deer's second-line defenses are critical and finely honed. They alert the whitetail to imminent danger and prompt it to take evasive action. The most effective of these defenses is the deer's sense of smell. If he sees you, a deer might snort, stamp and stare. After all, you could be another deer, even a swaying limb. Ditto if he hears you. You could be a squirrel, a cow or a nut falling. But if he smells you, the jig is up: Positive I.D., no questions asked, *bye bye* and flags are flying.

Compared to deer we humans are "olfactory-challenged," the nasal equivalent of being tone deaf. We don't even have a word to describe this inability to smell well. Blind, deaf, dumb and — what, smeaf? Just as we call deer "blind" when they fail to spot us sitting in plain sight, so might they shake their heads when we fail to smell them and think *We were stinking right in the open and those humans didn't even smell us! They must be so smeaf they can't smell the noses at the ends of their faces.* Thus deprived, we marvel at the amazing scenting talents of deer without even understanding their true magnitude. These animals can do with their noses what eagles can do with their eyes, what bats can do with their ears.

Any hunter who has spent a few days sitting in a stand has surely seen a whitetail come slipping along innocently until it reaches the path along which the hunter entered the field of battle. Instantly it slams to a stop as if it struck a glass wall. Up goes the head, forward go the ears, bulge go the eyes.

Depending on how ripe the lingering boot scent, the deer may immediately whirl and flee, crouch and slink away, or sniff long and carefully as if assessing the potential for mayhem. Sometimes, if the scent is old enough, the deer sniffs along as if to investigate the intruder. You can almost hear the wheels turning as the wary animal

deciphers the story. *Human. Two hours ago. Rubber boots. Pet dog. Gasoline. 200 pounds. 30 years old. Wife and two kids. Winchester Model 94! I'm outta here.* They're almost that good.

This nearly magical ability to "see" the world through nostrils is a result of a highly developed olfactory system beginning with that long snout. Like the air scoop on a race car, the bare, black external nose aids the flow of odors toward the inner nasal passages. There are no hairs to impede scent molecules, and deer regularly lick the smooth skin to "lubricate" odors. Before any substance can be smelled, it must be oxidized, released as a gas. Since most organic compounds are water-soluble, they adhere to or are absorbed by water molecules in the air. Thus, the water evaporating from a whitetail's naked nose helps capture organic gas molecules and transport them into the nasal passages where tissue rich in olfactory cells detects them. Nerves transport this information to the olfactory lobe of the brain. Message delivered, message deciphered.

Because of the length of their snouts, whitetails have roughly 100 times more "smelling" tissue than humans do. Whether this means they can smell 100 times better than humans is unproven. It may be that a whitetail's brain is more highly developed for scent discrimination, just as ours is more highly developed for reasoning. We may suck in the same odors, but are too "stupid" to recognize them. Science really has no way of measuring this. If we can't smell it, how do we know it's there, how intense it is? We also don't know if deer detect all subtle odors or are "dialed-in" for specific aromas. Meat eaters, for instance, are extremely sensitive to the stench of rotting flesh. Herbivores don't pay much attention to it, yet they can smell a bean under 6 inches of snow. Whitetails might be hypersensitive to the

Whitetails have exquisite olfactory powers. Just look at this buck testing the air currents for potential trouble.

Masking Odors

Can predators fool whitetails by masking their odors? Evidence is contradictory. Naturalists have long wondered whether coyotes and wolves roll in stench to disguise their own scent. Native Americans often stood in smoke before going on a hunt. Horsemen have reported riding right up to deer, disguised by the stench of their steeds. Today's hunters douse themselves and their equipment with fox urine, doe pee, skunk stink, anise oil, vanilla and untold dozens of homemade concoctions. Does any of this stuff work?

Probably not much. You might fool an inexperienced deer long enough to get a standing shot, but four-legged veterans of the hunt can sift and sort scents, finding the hunter's stink hidden even in a repugnant dose of skunk squirt. The best approach is to limit personal odors with unscented soaps and deodorants, clean rubber boots and clothes washed in unscented detergent. Use natural cover scents not to disguise odors, but to add a touch of realism and distraction. A deer that is busy deciphering faint traces of fox urine, raccoon urine, doe urine and acorn scent might overlook a whiff of hair oil.

body oils of predators, yet oblivious to the scent of ruffed grouse or lilies.

It's also likely that whitetails appear hypersensitive to odors because they are taught to detect and respond to them in ways we are not. Trained humans, such as perfume testers, can differentiate among nearly a thousand fragrances. The rest of us—bombarded with meaningless perfumes and harsh chemical odors daily—have to be reminded to stop, breathe deeply and recognize the scent of spring woods, rotting leaves or fresh-turned earth. Obviously, a fawn does not flee from the scent of a human until it is taught to do so. Such learning, coupled with perpetual heightened awareness, keeps deer tuned to critical odors the way humans are dialed in to flashing red lights.

To better understand a whitetail's scenting talents, think of odor molecules as musical notes. Each molecule has a slightly different tone, and deer can differentiate each of them much as a human with perfect pitch can differentiate C-sharp from C. For a visual comparison, imagine each molecule a color. Deer can smell pink from mauve, taupe from tan, ochre from burnt orange.

Regardless of what we know or don't know about *how well* deer smell, we do understand *why* they smell. Again, it's because of their environment. Any creature that opts to make its stand in thick cover has compromised vision and hearing. Foliage blocks the view, wind and noisy ground interfere with hearing. Trusting your sense of touch really puts you behind the eight ball: By the time you feel your enemy, he's upon you.

That leaves but one option—detecting airborne molecules that drift freely around leaves and branches irrespective of light levels and undiminished by competing sound waves. Over the ages, whitetails that scented best lived longest, and the deer among us today possess exquisite olfactory powers. Today a deer can stand several hundred yards downwind from a predator and, if the humidity is right, smell him plain as you could smell the Dodge City stockyards if you were standing in the middle of them.

Now Hear This

Sensitive as the whitetail's nose is, it can't overcome contrary winds. To protect its downwind side a deer relies heavily on its second most effective early warning system: its hearing. This is another defense ideally suited to life in the thick of it. Dense vegetation might muffle sound slightly and background noise might mask it, but generally sound waves carry well through typical whitetail habitat. Dry forest litter provides a convenient alarm against all but the lightest, quietest stalkers.

Because sound waves can be measured by machines, we have quantifiable evidence of a deer's superior hearing. Exceptionally sharp-eared humans detect sounds ranging from 20 to 20,000 cycles per second, but most adults lose sensitivity at both ends until they're mostly hearing things in the 40 to 16,000-cycle range. This is why the highest notes on a piano sound like dull plinks. We can't hear the ringing overtones. Deer can hear tones ranging from 20 to as high as 30,000 oscillations per second—the high, piercing kind dogs hear.

More importantly, whitetails can detect subtle sounds like cotton sleeves scraping against branches or padded feet striking wet ground. As with their sense of smell, good hearing may be as much learned as inherent. Because detecting approaching predators means the difference between life and death, deer learn early to tune in and stay tuned. They quickly sift background noise and inoffensive sounds from real trouble. They largely ignore scampering squirrels and rustling birds but recognize the unnatural rasp of nylon, the clunk of metal, the cadence of a walking human or the panting of a dog. They remain unflappable to the roar of passing traffic or distant gunshots, yet snap to attention at the breaking of a twig.

Even when asleep, whitetails keep their ears perked. Nearly 24 square inches of surface area make up each six-inch by three-inch cupped outer ear (the curve of the deep cup adds the extra area), and each of these auditory radar nets can be swiveled

With nearly 24 square inches of surface area on each ear, a buck can detect the most subtle sounds.

*A whitetail won't bound
off willy-nilly at the first
hint of danger. Like this
Wisconsin buck, he will
go on all-senses alert,
listening or smelling for
confirmation before
bolting.*

independently to front, side or rear like natural parabolic reflectors. To gain a frac-
tion of that ability, we must cup our hands behind our puny 6-inch-square ears. A
snoozing doe may twist her left ear backward at the crack of a twig without even
opening her eyes; if she hears a follow-up sound, she's awake and looking to confirm
her suspicions.

When they do hear a potentially threatening sound, deer rarely flee immediately.
Instead they go on full alert and search for confirmation. They may stand, head
high, ears forward, nose sniffing. Or they might prance cautiously, stiff-legged

toward the sound, trying to get visual contact. If they can't, they might circle downwind for an olfactory signal. Depending on how nervous or harried they are they may depart posthaste at the second suspicious sound or continue to seek corroboration. Older deer that have been hunted consistently may learn to bolt, no questions asked, at the click of a safety or even the squeak of a bow limb.

I CAN SEE CLEARLY NOW

As a defense from predators, a whitetail's vision is on par with its hearing: sharp but not independently trustworthy. This strikes humans as odd, given our almost total reliance on vision for detecting danger. With those big, dark eyes, how is it deer often can't see a human standing mere feet away?

Here again the whitetail's habitat and role as prey animal have shaped its abilities. Like most herbivorous ungulates, the whitetail has sacrificed color perception and some three-dimensional binocular vision for low light sensitivity and a broad field of view. Deer don't need to spy red apples from 400 yards to survive, but they do need to detect the slightest motion of a stalking predator at night. Thus, the whitetail's big eyes sit on the sides of its head and tilt about 24 degrees toward the front. They also bulge about a quarter of an inch beyond the skull. This positioning and extension clear most of the animal's own anatomy for a view of roughly 300 degrees. Though a whitetail can't see behind its head, it does seem that way. Thanks to the 24-degree forward angle, a whitetail also enjoys binocular vision and good depth perception across a relatively narrow 50-degree cone in front. This enables it to accurately gauge depth and distances for dodging and leaping over obstructions.

We might say that the whitetail sees so well at night because it's rod-rich and cone-poor. Rod cells lining the back of the eye (the retina) are highly reflective

BLAZE ORANGE

There will probably always be hunters who will resist wearing safety blaze orange and other bright colors, but there is no concrete evidence that such flashy garb spooks deer. Too many old bucks have nearly run over orange-clothed hunters over the years. By all accounts, deer see blaze orange as a light shade of gray, similar to a patch of sky, a white tree trunk or a boulder. That might make orange a more effective camouflage than dark camouflage patterns, especially in birch woods or atop a late-season treestand. As long as you don't dance a jig or stand in an open field, bright clothing shouldn't alert your quarry. Better to remain clearly identifiable to other hunters and take your chances with deer. Move slowly, stay low and break up your outline with natural cover: That's the trick.

and enhance low light at the expense of sharpness and color. This is why a deer's eyes glow under a spotlight. Cone cells, which humans have in abundance in the center of their retinas, detect color and sharpen vision, but fail miserably in low light. We have enough rod cells to get by in dim light, but you won't catch us running full tilt through a hardwood forest under cloud cover at midnight. Since whitetails are crepuscular (active at dusk and dawn) to nocturnal, rod cells make sense for them. Better to see the gray outline of a cougar when it's sneaking up on you in the dark than to spot its tawny pelt sleeping on a rock at noon. Besides, when the light dims, all colors shade to gray and black.

The upshot is that whitetails see only blurry forms in shades of gray but can detect the slightest motion, even in the darkest hours of the night. Thus, we can sit against an oak and watch amazed as a buck walks up, but if we lift an arm to draw a bow while a buck is quartering away at twilight, he'll often leap and run, having caught the motion in his peripheral vision.

This does not mean that predators can stand motionless in an open field or even on a woodland trail and become invisible to deer. Whitetails—especially cautious, hunted ones—may not know what that fuzzy object is, but they know it wasn't there yesterday. So they carefully investigate or they flee. An alert demeanor, intimate knowledge of their territory and healthy suspicion of anything new compensates for their lack of sharp color vision.

Pressured deer shy away as soon as they see something suspicious. But when the average deer sees something unusual, it may call on its other senses to corroborate. So it rivets its attention on the suspicious object, eyes wide, ears forward, nostrils testing the currents. The head bobs, a foreleg stamps the ground. The deer snorts loudly, trying to startle the potential predator into revealing itself. If that doesn't work, the deer often prances closer and tries again or circles cautiously to get your wind. Then, with a snort and a bound, it's gone.

A Good Defense is a Good Offense

A whitetail's standard response to perceived danger is flight, for which it is perfectly suited. When cover, camouflage and early warning systems fail, the philosophy is "hooves, don't fail me now." Usually, they don't.

The legs of a deer are designed for powerful acceleration using the principle of the lever. The bulk of the muscle on the rear leg is bunched high about the hip and pelvic girdle. The upper leg bone (femur) and lower leg bone (tibia) are relatively short while the foot is long and light; the bulky upper leg muscles can contract quickly and create powerful strokes that are magnified at the distant hoof. This

Opposite page: Once danger is confirmed and a whitetail goes, it really goes—tail up, legs churning, leaping over every obstacle.

A deer's legs are designed for powerful acceleration, using the principle of the lever.

converts power to speed much the way a fishing rod does, or a line of kids playing crack-the-whip.

Most people confuse a whitetail's hind foot with its lower leg. What looks like a "knee" that bends backward about halfway up a deer's rear leg is actually its ankle. The long bone below that joint is the metatarsus, equivalent to the metatarsal bones in our feet. It has been fused and lengthened to create a strong cannon bone that provides increased leverage and speed for running and jumping. Additional leverage comes from the two elongated middle toes tipped with hooves. The "big toe" is gone entirely, the first and last digits are the dew claws higher up: The whitetail actually walks and runs on tiptoe, much as a human sprinter does to achieve top speed.

The front legs are similar. What looks like the knee or elbow joint is really the "wrist" joint. All that long bone below it is the metacarpal: another single, fused cannon bone equivalent to our hand bones between our wrists and fingers. Above this are the radius and ulna bones that correspond to our forearms, then the "elbow" behind which hunters like to aim for a heart shot. The deer's "shoulder" is really its upper arm, or humerus, and its scapula, or shoulder blade. Again, the driving muscles are concentrated around these two upper bones: this propels the light, long lower leg and foot both powerfully and rapidly.

These special designs give the whitetail its impressive speed and leaping ability. When alarmed, a deer usually trots with head up and erect tail wagging. Depending on its fright, it may travel anywhere from 5 to 12 mph. If it's really spooked, it breaks into a full gallop at 20 to 40 mph with bounds as long as 29 horizontal feet. As a rule, a frightened whitetail will streak downhill and toward dense cover where it will look for a place to hide. Wary old bucks often wait and watch their backtrails or circle to get behind their pursuers.

STAND & DELIVER

When all else fails, our timid whitetail will stand and fight, but only as a last resort. One exception is the doe driving coyotes away from her fawns. If a coyote or bobcat wanders within the nursery area, an aggressive doe will trot right toward them and strike with her front hooves or attempt to chase the predators from the area. Later in the summer, when several does and fawns have formed extended family herds, the old does will challenge coyotes en masse. When a single doe or buck is cornered by wolves or coyotes, it will slash with its front hooves. If bucks have polished antlers, they'll lower their heads and attempt to spear their antagonists. Sometimes they'll even succeed. Usually, however, truly serious predators will prevail—especially when there is more than one to harass and attack the deer's flanks. At that point the individual deer cashes in his or her chips, and the whitetail's final, perhaps most effective predatory defense takes over.

REPRODUCE & FLOURISH

Reproduction. That's the key. Against constant pressures from numerous predators, no deer can hope to die of old age. Thus the species' best defense against extermination is consistent and successful production of offspring. If enough fawns are born each spring, populations replenish themselves, replace the embattled old bucks too weak to fend off wolves, the venerable does no longer fast enough to dodge bobcats and cougars, the young bucks too inexperienced to avoid hunters. An individual deer, then, doesn't have to live forever—just long enough to produce a replacement. Based on how the whitetail population has increased in the U.S. since the turn of the century, many are succeeding. Given the right habitat, whitetails have all the tools needed to survive and thrive.

This farm-country fawn is less than a week old. This particular deer may not make it to adulthood, but enough fawns will to continue the species.

PELAGE

DRESSED FOR SUCCESS

Newborn fawns hide where their mothers tell them to, camouflaged and nearly odorless. They won't move unless they're almost touched.

Perhaps the least exciting part of a whitetail is its coat. No fancy stripes, no elaborate napes, goatees, bells or whistles. Just your basic wash-and-wear brown suit. Never needs ironing; works in rain, sun or snow. Guaranteed for less than a year, but replacements are free for life.

Each deer's first coat is its prettiest: a lovely, soft red sprinkled with hundreds of bright white dots over the back and sides. This beautiful pelt, ironically, isn't meant to be seen. It is designed to blend with the dappled light of a young forest. The spots fade as the fawn grows, and by November, the first winter coat has replaced the spotted one once and for all.

Adult summer coats are a similar red color. The inch-long hairs, roughly 5,000 per square inch, are smooth, straight and fine. There is no underfur. The winter coat, grown in about one month beginning in late August or September, is tan to gray-brown, but sports only about 2,600 hairs per square inch. What? Less hair for winter wear? Sure. This creates insulating dead air space. Each hair is 2 inches long and kinked along its length; the

HORSE DEER?

One of the rarest pelt conditions among whitetails is a mane. Sometimes this is just the usual 2-inch hairs standing erect in a narrow band from the head down to the shoulders, but sometimes these ridge hairs are as long as those on a horse's mane. This does not represent a cross between a whitetail doe and a stallion; just another genetic mutation. Nature tests all sorts of things from time to time, just in case conditions are ripe for them to succeed.

An adult whitetail's coat is red in the summer and changes to gray-brown for fall and winter.

kinks create the air pockets. In addition, each hair is spongy inside, containing more air pockets. And at the base of these long guard hairs, which are oily enough to be fairly waterproof, is the underfur: a fluffy blanket of fine, bent, wool-like hairs. So efficient a thermal blanket is a whitetail's winter pelt that snow collects atop it without melting.

This amazingly effective hide does not extend down the animal's legs, where hairs remain short and straight. Yet, as any hunter who has nearly frozen his toes knows, the extremities are the first to suffer. So how does a whitetail keep its feet warm? Mostly it doesn't. A deer has minimal living tissue, including nerves, below its ankles and wrists. The arteries and veins in a whitetail's legs are wrapped in a

Northern whitetails have evolved to survive harsh winters. This young deer even looks comfortable in the cold snow.

layer of insulating fat. Fresh, outbound blood heats returning veinous blood to protect the core temperature. Simultaneously, veinous blood cools outgoing blood so that precious body heat is not lost. Toward the hooves, temperatures are downright chilly, but a deer apparently doesn't feel it, having evolved to handle such conditions. Frostbite is the curse of humans who rushed out of their equatorial birthplace protected by artificial insulation. There's been darn little natural selection for frost-free limbs among us.

Slow Shed

Although it only takes about four weeks for a deer to grow its winter coat, the summer coat is months in coming. The old winter rug might slowly begin shedding as early as March. Old hair begins falling from the face and head first, progressing down the body. The real disrobing begins in May but can continue into July—little more than a month before the new winter coat starts showing. Growth depends on overall health: The more robust the deer, the sooner and more quickly it grows its new coat.

FEW COLOR OPTIONS

When it comes to color, whitetails are a bit like early Ford automobiles which could be ordered in any color—as long as it was black. Well, our deer aren't quite that monochromatic. While they're all basically brown-gray in winter and reddish in summer, northern animals are somewhat darker than southern specimens, forest-dwelling deer darker than open-country deer, and desert deer paler than woodland deer. All whitetails have bright white bellies that extend from the brisket between the front legs back to the tip of the tail. On most, the white extends down the insides of the rear legs and the back edge of the front legs to the ankle or wrist joints, tapering to a point. The insides of the ears are filled with long white hairs, and each eye is encircled by white. The only other white is on the front half of the muzzle extending down to the throat, where there is a sizable white throat patch. A deer rarely has two throat patches separated by a band of normal, dark hairs.

The exceptions to this standard color pattern are genetically white pelts, piebald hides and rare melanistic or albino skins. Each of these color schemes is a genetic anomaly that has always been coursing through the whitetails' veins. It occasionally pops up, just in case conditions have changed to favor such an unusual outer coating. Melanistic pelts are nearly black because of overproduction of melanin, the body's coloring pigment. Albinism, of course, is due to an absence of melanin.

White deer are fairly common in some parts of the East, where they have been protected from shooting by local or state laws—a rather silly arrangement that favors a genetic mutation over nature's more effective brown-coated deer. When four-legged predators return to these areas and discover the "protected" white deer, populations will suffer because wolves and cougars pay little attention to game laws.

A Michigan albino fawn with its normal-colored mother.

*A Florida whitetail
emerges from the forest
to feed in a field during
late afternoon.*

DIGESTIVE SYSTEM

DIGEST THIS

If it were literally true that you are what you eat, whitetails would be green. And nutty. And woody, corny and flowery. In other words, they eat darn near anything—including, but not limited to, grass, leaves, buds, forbs, sedges, wildflowers, weeds, grain, mushrooms, fruit, nuts, roots, algae, fish and ladybugs. This is partly why they're so successful and widespread. They thrive in oak woods because they eat acorns. They survive in northern conifer forests because, when snow covers other forage, they eat white cedar boughs. In southern pine woods they find just enough understory plants and forbs to get by. Irrigated grains and alfalfa enabled them to migrate deep into the Plains states. They do well even in places like northern Illinois, where fall plowing buries about 90 percent of all vegetative cover: They survive on scraps of woodland and native browse until summer brings a rebirth of new crops.

PICKY, PICKY, PICKY

Despite this diet, whitetails are considered selective feeders (browsers) as opposed to bulk grazers like bison. Deer try to select the most nutritious, easily digestible plant material available—vegetation high in soluble protein, fats and carbohydrates but relatively low in fiber. This diet is predicted by the shapes of their faces. Bulk grazers such as bison and cattle have relatively short, broad muzzles designed to mow off big swaths of grass with each bite. If you're not fussy about what you eat, this tactic is quite efficient. Whitetails' long, narrow muzzles more effectively reach and pluck nutritious tidbits from among less useful vegetation (while keeping eyes and ears clear to scan for predators) as they browse along. In this way the whitetail is a picky eater. It picks a sweet cloverleaf here, a dandelion blossom there, and an acorn while avoiding tufts of coarse, dry grass that would just fill it up without providing much nutrition.

BELLY BUDDIES

The reason for such selective feeding has to do with the deer's amazing four-chambered stomach. The rumen, reticulum, omasum and abomasum are not just acid vats in which food is broken down. They're zoos, fermentation plants and execution pits. Billions of bacteria, protozoa and other microorganisms live and breed in a whitetail's rumen and reticulum, eating rough plant material, and converting it to fatty acids that the deer can absorb. Billions of these helpful bacteria get swept along through the plumbing where they, too, are digested and absorbed, a clear cut case of biting the hand that feeds you.

But pity not the poor bacteria. Without the deer's rumen to call home, they wouldn't be able to survive. Besides, the billions sliding to their demise down the nether reaches of the whitetail's intestinal tract have had ample time to divide and multiply, leaving behind billions of replicas of themselves to carry on. Thus the whitetail and its gut microflora enjoy a classic symbiotic relationship, each benefiting from its association with the other.

GASTRIC TIDBITS

Depending on its digestibility, vegetation may remain in a whitetail's rumen and reticulum for a few hours or several days. Up to 10 percent of a deer's live weight is vegetation currently undergoing digestion. Eighty percent of that takes place in the rumen, which does most of the work breaking down the plants. In each gram of rumen material there are about 50 billion bacteria and 500,000 protozoa. These critters, in conjunction with internal body heat of about 104°F, convert vegetation into a variety of fatty acids that are absorbed by the papillae to provide some 40 percent of the deer's energy requirements.

Contractions of the stomach walls mix the mash and, when pieces are small enough, push them into the omasum. Here water, minerals and some products of fermentation are absorbed. By the time the omasum contents reach the final chamber, the abomasum, they've been turned into green slurry. Here hydrochloric acid, pepsin and rennin are added to the mix. The abomasum absorbs certain nutrients, then sends the slurry into the 49-foot-long small intestine where most of the nutrient absorption takes place. Enzymes from the pancreas and intestine plus liver bile attack starches, lipids and proteins. The end products are absorbed by the small intestine walls. The large intestine absorbs a limited amount of fatty acids, minerals and vitamins and most of the remaining water, compacts what remains into pellets or clumps, and passes this waste as the pellets we hunters love to find and examine.

Sexual Segregation By Belly Size

Male ungulates often live apart from females except during breeding season. But why? Relative gut size may hold at least part of the answer. Because whitetail bucks are usually about one-third larger than does, bucks have correspondingly larger rumen capacities and can therefore process a higher volume of lesser-quality forage while maintaining body condition and good health. By foraging away from does and fawns, bucks can find plenty to eat without having to compete with the more numerous females and their young. This may be why older bucks in the Northeast often winter on the fringes of traditional deer yards where forage quality is lower but quantity sometimes higher.

Despite their microflora colonies, whitetails still can't digest really coarse cellulose, due to the relatively small volume of their first two stomach chambers coupled with the structure of their linings. An efficient cellulose eater, such as a Holstein cow, has a huge rumen lined with hundreds of thousands of papillae—short projections of the stomach lining that look like a mass of little worms. Papillae increase the absorptive surface area of the stomach.

Whitetails have smaller rumens than those of cattle and fewer and shorter papillae. Look at a whitetail and a cow head-on and you get an idea of the differences in their gut sizes. Notice how much farther the cow bulges to each side? Rumen capacity. Cows need this in order to process enough low-energy, high-fiber grass to thrive. The downside is their extra bulk and weight makes them relatively slow and easy for predators to catch. Whitetails, by keeping rumen volume low, remain light on their feet and one jump ahead of the wolf. The tradeoff is they must high-grade their food selection.

An Open & Closed Case

Large herbivores face choices. They can live in the open, or in the closed cover of the forest. Or they can divide their time between the two. The more time they spend in the open, the greater the odds they'll be spotted by a predator. In self defense they join into herds on the principle that 40 eyes are better than two. The more open the habitat, the larger the herd. But the larger the herd, the greater the demand on forage.

Fortunately, open country is usually carpeted in grass that can withstand heavy grazing because of its extensive root system. (Blades grow from their bottoms up. Nip off the leaf and it just keeps sprouting.) But grass is also relatively high in silica and difficult to digest. So grazers need large rumens in order to process enough forage. That makes them heavier, slower and easier to catch, which is another reason they live in herds in the open where they can see trouble coming from a long way off.

Because whitetails spend most of their lives in dense cover, they take a different approach. The shrubs, vines, trees and forbs they eat grow from their tips. Nip them off and growth stops until the plant can force another bud below the lost limb. Often regrowth doesn't begin until the next spring. Shrubs and forbs cannot withstand as much grazing pressure as grasses, so whitetails can't live in large herds. But woodland foliage, nuts, fruits and wildflowers are more nutritious than grasses, so a deer can survive with a smaller rumen as long as it searches out the best forage available in each season.

This daily search for the perfect food also keeps deer out of the grasp of their enemies. A whitetail eats gourmet takeout on the run. It grabs a bite here, steps forward, sniffs out an acorn there, lifts its head, pulls down a leaf, turns it head, spies a mushroom, and walks five steps to pluck that. With all this activity the deer is constantly stepping into new scent streams, seeing new perspectives and moving away from any predators stalking from behind. A cow or bison simply puts its nose to the ground and munches. It can afford to. If it doesn't see, hear or smell the approaching wolf, its herd mates probably will.

THE CHANGING MENU

Not surprisingly, the microflora in a whitetail's gut is different from that in a cow's gut, and each is optimized to break down the consumed plant materials efficiently. Nevertheless, a whitetail's gut microorganisms change gradually over the course of a year to accommodate seasonal shifts in diet. Fresh, protein-rich spring growth, for instance, requires different bacteria than does dry, high-cellulose winter browse. This explains why starving deer fed emergency hay in hard winters often die with their bellies full: Bacteria that have been breaking down cedar branches and dog-wood twigs for two months can't handle the sudden influx of alfalfa or grain. But the deer, knowing a good thing when they taste it, pig out on the new food, unwit-tingly violating their contract with their internal partners. With the supply of woody browse suddenly gone, the old microflora die out and the new bacteria haven't time to build up to viable production levels. The poor deer sits with a belly full of indigestible forage.

Yet deer have an unexplained ability to identify and select vegetation that has the highest concentrations of soluble cell material, and, in these cases, they can suddenly change their preferred forage. For instance, when acorns fall, deer eat

A whitetail will change its menu with the seasons. This buck happens to be a Florida Key deer standing on his hind legs to nip some succulent browse.

CHEW ON THIS

The hunter was excited after shooting a good-sized buck with a hefty rack. "I'll bet he's an old one," he said to his admiring companions. Then he lifted the buck's upper front lip and peered into its mouth. "Oh my gosh, look at this!" The young man ran his fingers over the buck's upper gums. "It's so old it doesn't even have any teeth up here. They're worn clear down to the gums!"

Well, not really. His buck never did have teeth in the front of its upper jaw. No deer ever does. Instead whitetails have a tough pad of skin against which vegetation is pressed while the lower incisors nip it off. You have to look nearly halfway back on a deer's upper jaw before seeing its line of grinding teeth: three premolars and three molars per side. The lower jaw sports six incisors and two canine teeth up front with a toothless gap of gum between those and the premolars and molars—again three of each per side to match their upper counterparts. These are the crucial grinding surfaces used to masticate and pulverize tough forage.

A deer's teeth are key to the animal's survival, the critical first stage of the digestion process. Without them a deer starves. Grinding teeth typically wear down about one millimeter each year, so by the time a whitetail is 10 or 11, its teeth are worn to the gums. At that point a deer will slowly starve unless it can find sufficient soft forage high in soluble nutrients that can be digested with minimum chewing.

Annual growth rings or cementum layers appear in the roots of a deer's incisors, much like growth rings on a tree. A tooth can be sliced thin, stained and the rings counted to accurately age the deer. A few whitetails have been aged at 20 years, but in the wild few make it past ten.

acorns. And on the plains they shift from alfalfa to winter wheat as soon as new wheat shoots emerge. These changes are not as drastic as emergency winter feeding behavior (see the winter section, pages 178–191). Just how whitetails can so quickly zero in on these premium crops is a mystery, but an essential survival trick for such selective feeders.

EATING SAFELY

In one respect a whitetail's stomach resembles a chipmunk's cheek pouches. It permits the deer to capture and store its food quickly, then retire to relative safety to "eat" it later. This minimizes the animal's vulnerable period of exposure. Instead of standing and chewing for hours, constantly distracted by ripping and swaying vegetation, a whitetail nips off a mouthful of goodies, gives them two or four token chews, and swallows. Within 2 hours it generally fills its 8-quart rumen capacity and can slip back into heavy cover. Here it can watch, smell and listen for trouble while it re-chews its meal. Muscles in the rumen and esophagus contract to push up a cud or bolus of partially digested material about the size of a hen's egg. Folks who've taken the time to count claim that the average whitetail masticates each

This Wisconsin buck lies in a hardwood forest chewing his cud, a digestive adaptation that lets him eat quickly and then return to cover.

A group of whitetails feeding in the early morning fog. As the sun rises, the deer will slowly melt back into thick vegetation to bed and ruminate.

cud about 46 times with a side-to-side grinding action. The object is to break the vegetation into tiny pieces. This exposes more surface area to rumen/reticulum bacteria, increasing fermentation efficiency.

THE FEEDING CYCLE

While most hunters understand that whitetails slip from their daytime beds at dusk to begin feeding, many don't know how long the animals actually forage. If prime food is abundant, such as a lush wheat field or heavy fall of acorns, a deer can fill up in an hour. If pickings are few and far between, it may wander and gather what it can for three hours or more. This is partly why at midday you sometimes see whitetails foraging during February in the north or August during southern droughts.

Foraging time also depends on the deer's sex. As most hunters know, does and fawns generally feed later in the morning and start earlier in the afternoon than do bucks, even where both sexes are hunted. Females also forage more frequently throughout the day, often rising every two or three hours to wander and feed lightly for an hour, then bedding another two or three hours, then rising to snack again. It isn't until late afternoon that they march purposefully toward a crop field, meadow or acorn hotspot for a serious meal. After one to three hours of pigging out, depending on forage quality and quantity, they bed—usually right where they've been feeding if it's dark, or in nearby cover if it's still light. They rise to feed for an hour or so at about 10 p.m. and again at 2 a.m. Near dawn they feed heavily. In spring and fall they may stay at it until midmorning before trekking toward dense bedding cover.

Bucks are less active and more cautious. In summer they may not step into open feeding areas until dark. In late autumn and winter they're usually eating at sunset or as much as an hour before. Since they have larger stomachs to fill, they feed for a good three hours, especially after the rut when they must replenish lost fat. Surprisingly, even old, wary bucks will lie down to ruminate in the middle of a wheat or alfalfa field at night. Darkness alone provides enough cover to make them comfortable. They've even been observed feeding while lying down, craning their long necks to crop all vegetation within reach. Like does, they'll rise about 10 p.m. for a serious round of refilling, then bed until the 2 a.m. feeding, then bed again until nearly dawn. Depending on hunting pressure, season, temperatures, and forage quality and abundance, bucks may strike out for daytime beds at the crack of dawn or feed until an hour after sunup.

En route to bedding cover a buck will often swipe a morsel or pause to browse a tasty plant for several minutes. The better the woodland browse, the sooner a buck will leave open feeding areas and the longer it will linger along its bedroom trail. But if hunting pressure makes him cautious and he's filled up on nutritious cereal crops or fresh, green browse, he'll step smartly toward the security of his day bed. Here he lies calmly and may not rise until noon for a stretch. After voiding he often nibbles nearby for an hour. Then it's back to the "couch" for a lazy afternoon of chewing cud and watching for predators.

When disturbed regularly by predators, deer easily shift their schedules to avoid conflict. Bucks especially will abandon all daylight activity and forage only at night. Buck activity levels often rise for two or three hours around midday, when hunters routinely knock off for lunch and a nap.

It usually takes about 14 hours for forage to progress through the reticulum, another 10 to 16 hours for it to pass through the rest of the system. To maintain its culture of microflora, a whitetail stokes its rumen with a mixture of plants. Although it might concentrate on wheat leaves or corn kernels or apples, it will grab a few bites of this and that to maintain a broader population of bacteria and pick up vitamins, trace minerals, proteins and carbohydrates.

A Montana buck heading for cover after a night of feeding. Depending on the forage along the way, he may pause for a few bites before reaching his bedding cover.

COMMUNICATIONS

A goose honks loudly when it loses its flock. A wolf howls to declare its territory. But a whitetail lives practically at a whisper. Being the object of so many predators, it can't afford to advertise itself too blatantly. Yet females somehow keep track of their fawns, bucks steer clear of other bucks and hot lovers manage to rendezvous. Obviously whitetails are communicating. But how?

OLFACTORY LANGUAGE

NOSING OUT THE ANSWERS

As this mature buck demonstrates, smelling is the strongest communicative sense.

Like humans, whitetails communicate via five senses: sight, sound, smell, touch and taste. The strongest of these is smell, as suggested by the various scent glands scattered over a deer's body. Using gland odors, urine and sometimes droppings, whitetails send and receive scent messages much the way we do written notes and letters. They even maintain post offices, of sorts.

The most prominent whitetail scent glands are the pair of tarsals, one on the inside of each hind leg at the bend of the ankle. During the rut, 3-inch-wide tufts of long, stiff hair surrounding these glands are stained and stinky, and not just from the oily lactones the glands secrete. Most of the smell emanates from the urine each deer intentionally deposits by squatting with its hind legs together, tarsal tufts

often rubbing together as the urine runs over them. This is how bucks anoint their ground scrapes during the rut. When deer meet, each sniffs the other's tarsal glands much the way dogs nose one another's rear ends, a practice that suggests each deer exudes a personal tarsal perfume.

META-MYSTERY

The metatarsal glands are curious tufts of hair on the outside, lower hind legs that prove just how little we really know about whitetails. Unlike the tarsals, they do not produce an obvious oil or secretion (although some observers swear they have a slight garlic smell). Whitetails do not urinate upon their metatarsals or rub them against anything, so they pretty much have us baffled. Blacktails and mule deer reportedly flare their metatarsals, which are considerably longer than those of whitetails, to release a warning scent. This function may have atrophied among whitetails. Some scientists suggest that metatarsals are used to regulate body temperature and have nothing to do with producing odors. If biologists are this far apart, you can bet they're mostly guessing, which is nothing to be ashamed of. Throughout history man has begun his investigations of the natural world by guessing, then observing and testing to prove or disprove his suspicions.

TOEING THE LINE

Less obvious but more significant than metatarsals are the interdigital glands found between the toes of each foot just above the hooves. Spread the toes wide, pull back the hair and you'll find a narrow pocket lined with sparse, short, stiff hairs. Numerous sweat glands within the skin emit a slightly yellow wax that apparently

GROOMING

Does commonly lick (groom) their fawns, and fawns lick back. This is typical social behavior among herding mammals that tightens the bonds that maintain group cohesiveness. But we don't see much mutual grooming between mature does or bucks because whitetails are generally loners, or at best, casual associates. Nevertheless, summer bucks that spend a lot of time together do occasionally groom one another, and does will often groom previous years' fawns as well as their new young 'uns. Forced herding such as found in winter yards also increases mutual grooming.

carries a unique cachet. With each step a deer writes its signature in stink. This allows fawns and does to relocate their family groups and helps bucks track down does. When a nervous whitetail stamps a forefoot, prances dramatically or flees with pounding hoofs, it lays down sudden "splashes" of interdigital scent which might serve as olfactory red flags. *Look out gang! Proceed with caution.* To avoid unhealthy attention, spotted fawns probably do not develop interdigital scent until they are several weeks old and strong enough to run from predators.

EYE WAS HERE

Preorbital glands, sometimes called lachrymal glands, are those inch-long grooves or pockets of nearly hairless skin outside the lower front corner of a deer's eyes. They appear to be tear ducts modified for scent production because they lie outside the moist inner eyelids and exude a waxy substance instead of tears. Mule deer flare their preorbitals when startled or threatened, suggesting dispersal of an alarm or threat scent. But whitetails don't appear to do this. Instead, bucks carefully rub this gland on licking branches and twigs at scrape sites.

Although preorbitals don't have a powerful odor, some humans can detect a slight ammonia scent. Whitetails, with their superior olfactory powers, probably smell this "loud and clear." Surely the glands send some kind of message because other deer sniff these twigs before marking them too. Probably it's a personal identification scent, a deer's way of staying in touch. This makes licking branches, which all passing deer appear to check and mark, comparable to stopping by a post office or bulletin board.

You can see the pre-orbital gland in front of this alert buck's eye.

Preorbital glands are obvious and important scent producers for many ungulate species. Subordinate Dall sheep rub their noses and horn tips over the preorbital glands of dominant rams, perhaps to identify themselves as part of his bachelor band to prevent unwanted aggression. Muskoxen ooze preorbital secretions as a personal marking scent and wipe them aggressively across their forelegs when challenging other males during the rut. The white faces of blesbok antelope in Africa are heavily stained by yellow preorbital gland secretions. Little dik-dik antelope mark territorial boundaries with preorbital scent. Odds are good that whitetails use their preorbital scent as personal markers too. But because our own scenting powers are so weak, we may never know for sure.

RUBS A-HEAD

The whitetail's forehead scent gland is a recent and important discovery. For decades, field observers were suspicious because so much antler rubbing looked more like forehead rubbing. Finally, in the early 1980s, researchers began examining the forehead skin of bucks and does during various seasons. Sure enough, the scalp between the antler base and upper eye harbors numerous odor-producing glands in both sexes. These enlarge significantly during the rut, especially in older bucks. The bigger and more dominant the buck, the darker his forehead and the more he rubs it against bushes, saplings and trees to make his olfactory mark. Perhaps it's a warning that decreases the libido of other bucks; possibly it's an invitation that increases the libido of neighborhood does. Could be a bit of both.

During the rut, dominant bucks rub their foreheads on branches and trees, leaving scent signposts. This buck's forehead patch is getting dark from the activity.

BACK UP

The little-known supercaudal gland sits atop the whitetail's back near the base of the tail, but we can only guess at its function. In some mammals, oil from this gland is used during grooming to waterproof fur. Pronghorns flare the hairs over their supercaudal glands when alarmed, perhaps releasing a warning scent—but pronghorn bucks also raise these hairs when courting does. What whitetails do with supercaudal glands only they know, and so far they aren't telling.

ORAL FIXATIONS

Recently biologists discovered nasal scent glands in whitetails, and there may be some in the mouth too. How else to explain the way bucks approach licking branches? They smell, lick, chew on and pull the branch through their mouths like a child licking a milkshake straw. Sometimes they poke it into their nostrils. Clearly they are detecting and/or leaving some sort of chemical message. Maybe the odor of their saliva is sufficient to identify them; maybe the saliva enhances the power of the preorbital cologne. Here's yet another mystery we wish we could sniff out.

URINE & YEAR OUT

Whitetails send messages through their urine and perhaps their droppings. Bucks, of course, urinate down their tarsal glands and into their scrapes. This probably warns other bucks just how mature, strong and dangerous the depositor is; the message—keep your distance! It might also dampen their enthusiasm, even their physiological readiness, to breed. The longer a buck lives and the bigger he gets, the more his

urine-soaked tarsals stink. Bucks also sniff fresh doe urine and curl their upper lips in the famous Flehmen posture, the better to determine breeding status. When the female's perfume hits a specific "tone," the male's nose knows. And to make sure the boys find her passionate "love letters," the doe begins cruising her territory incessantly, dribbling a quick note here and another there.

Because humans don't "smell" the whitetail language, we don't know precisely what messages our favorite deer are communicating with their various glands and body odors. We do know that they are not strictly territorial; bucks do not defend a plot of home ground from other bucks. Rather, they defend their position in the social order. So odds are high that many of the whitetail's odors are designed to convey individual identity, sexual status, perhaps age (which correlates strongly with size and rank), relative health and, ultimately, social standing. It's no accident that the biggest, dominant buck in the neighborhood also happens to be the stinkiest.

The typical scrape is located under an overhanging branch that the buck licks, chews, rubs, horns and generally marks with his scent.

BODY LANGUAGE

TAILS YOU LOSE

Like most large mammals, whitetails use and read body language fluently. The most familiar visual whitetail signal is the raised, flared, waving white tail. Clearly it signals danger and practically shouts "Run!" Does almost always flee with flags flying, probably to show their fawns the way to safety, perhaps to taunt or confuse predators and encourage them to abandon the hunt. Research of similar tail flaring by a number of deer species worldwide indicates that its main function is just that—informing the predator that it has been detected.

Sometimes bucks flag, sometimes they don't. Years ago most hunters thought that if a buck dropped its tail while running it was hit; if the tail was up, it had been missed. That's not always true. Most older bucks run with a low tail whether hit, missed or not even shot at. We assume they don't want to draw attention to themselves.

Besides danger, whitetail tails tell other tales. A briskly wriggling tail is a sure sign of a fawn enjoying its milk meal. When a deer stops feeding or walking to watch alertly, head up, it will always flick its tail before resuming its routine.

This corn-fed buck shows the most famous visual sign of a whitetail in flight: a raised, flared and waving tail. It's a visual warning to other whitetails in the area, and possibly a message to predators that the game's over: "I'm gone. You lose."

Unfortunately for predators, the tail projects no similar warning before snapping back to attention. A buck walking with its head down and tail half-cocked is scent-trailing a doe. A nervous whitetail slowly flares its white rump hairs and gradually elevates its tail. As the suspicion grows, so does the tail, until it and the white derriere create a bright banner designed to warn other deer.

HEADS UP

When a whitetail is curious, but not necessarily fearful, it usually stands to face the object of suspicion, neck and head level with or slightly below the backline, ears and nose forward. Then it bobs its head up and down, side-to-side like a boxer, as if trying to see around the creature or startle it into moving. This body language signals other deer. They know something interesting has been uncovered and they prance over to help investigate. If, however, a deer thinks it has detected a possible predator, it snaps its head high, cocks its ears forward and stares in the classic heads-up posture. Nearby deer will turn to stare in the same direction. As suspicions rise they stamp a forefoot, flare rump hairs, perhaps step forward and snort.

EAR YE EAR YE

A deer's ears function much like semaphore flags, displaying intentions and spelling out predictions of what's going to happen next. Aimed forward they telegraph

alertness or, when coupled with erect head and intent staring, possible danger. Ears held back and upward, combined with averted eyes and a humped back or lowered hind quarters, signal submission. Dropping the hindquarters or squatting is a common sign of deference among ungulates, much like slinking among dogs. The reduction in size is an obvious capitulation to a superior force. It may also diffuse aggression and halt attacks by mimicking the helpless dependence of a fawn.

Coupled with a low, outstretched neck and a direct stare, laid-back ears represent anger or aggression, threatening an imminent chase or a standing foreleg kick. The same ear position with the head up predicts a rearing, flailing attack with both front feet.

Any leg kick is a clear sign of dominance. It may be a simple upward whack under the brisket or belly, an overhead chop to the neck or back, or a full-fledged, stallion-like rearing double kick. The kickee usually cocks its ears back, squats and moves away in a classic act of submission. But sometimes it will challenge with a kick of its own, resulting in a few seconds of vertical kickboxing before one of the contestants backs down. Generally bachelor groups and matriarchal societies know one another well enough that the dominance hierarchy is clear, changing only when older animals die or younger ones grow bigger and stronger than the others. Yearlings assume some of the rank of their dams, thus the fawns of a high-ranking doe will dominate the fawns of a less dominant doe.

When bucks wish to project superiority and dominance, they approach opponents stiff-legged with ears not only laid back but also pressed down along the neck. The tail is clamped down and the body hairs flared like a cat dropped in front of a strange dog. This "bad hair day" look enlarges overall appearance and imparts a dark, menacing body color. A threatening buck with hard antlers also lowers its chin so as to project its tines forward, an obvious sign of clear and present danger. A submissive buck has only to look or turn away to diffuse the situation. If he stares back or faces the aggressive buck, trouble's brewing.

A direct stare is such a blatant threat among whitetails that bucks, to avoid any possible misinterpretation, routinely bed facing in different directions. That practice not only prevents internal squabbles but also strengthens the defensive line against sneak attack.

ADVANCED COMMUNICATIONS

At least one visual communication tool that whitetails employ does not involve body language. It's the autumnal tree rub. No one can prove this, but biologists believe that when a buck strips the bark off a tree with his antlers and rubs the bare wood with his forehead glands, he's proclaiming his presence and intent. *I'm here, I'm big and I'm aggressive. Best stay out of my way.* Rubs are roughly analogous to the high school jock draping his letter jacket over his girlfriend. The warning may not deter every randy competitor, but it'll discourage many, give pause to others, and dampen the enthusiasm of all but the biggest and most confident. This theory supports the observation that the bigger the buck, the bigger the rub.

Above: A buck approaches another with ears laid back, body hair flattened, and staring, glaring eyes. This is obviously a dominant buck that means business! Most subordinate bucks will avoid eye contact to diffuse this situation. Left: Large bucks often rub large saplings, creating stark, white signposts advertising their presence.

Vocal Communication

Deer Talk

Quiet though they may be, whitetails are not mute. In fact, researchers have identified about a dozen distinct vocal signals, most of them subtle variations of grunts, bleats and whines that say everything from *Back off* to *Come on baby, light my fire*.

The whitetail's only truly loud call is the familiar warning snort that informs predators that the jig is up and alerts other deer to lurking danger. Nearly as loud is the frightened bawl of a deer, usually a fawn, caught in the clutches of a predator. A bawl usually brings does running to the defense and galvanizes all whitetails within hearing. Even bucks will often stand up to see what the fuss is about or approach to investigate.

A buck's rutting grunts carry fairly well on a calm day. While following a nearly ripe doe, a buck often grunts with each step as if he can barely contain his joy, sounding remarkably like a happy pig. The sounds are guttural and wholly unromantic to humans, but whitetail does probably hear them as tender sweet nothings.

Other buck grunts sound more amphibian than mammalian—low pitched, toad-like aaaaaahs, burps and sudden growling clicks. When two males meet in a testosterone venting contest, they're likely to whine or snort-wheeze, clearly audible threats which sound something like blasts of escaping steam.

Does call their fawns with soft, cat-like mews, and lost fawns bleat for rescue. These and similar "staying in touch" calls are usually so soft that humans don't hear them unless they are within a few yards of the deer. Does probably also command tender fawns to lie down and remain hidden when predators approach.

A Call to Arms

One sound that is not meant to send a message or call other deer nevertheless does just that. It's the click and crash of antlers when bucks fight. After velvet shedding but before actual breeding begins, bucks spend a lot of time sparring to sort out the pecking order. Like any good sporting event, the click and clack of a sparring match draws an audience. Later, as bachelor parties break up and does near their estrus, overanxious bucks sometimes tangle like drunks at a redneck bar, desperate to prove who's more macho. When such rows erupt, testosterone and curiosity drive every other buck within hearing to run in and watch—if not join—the action.

Opposite page: Bucks don't fight often, but when they do, it is a sight to behold. These northwoods bucks are in the middle of an all-out dominance struggle; one could even die.

BUCKSNORT?

Years ago many hunters believed that only bucks snorted. "I heard a buck snort!" was a common brag in northwoods hunting camps. We now know better. These days some hunters claim they can tell the difference between a buck and doe snort. Can they? Maybe. Because a buck is some 20 to 30 percent larger than the average doe, it has a correspondingly larger trachea, nostrils and lung capacity. This could translate into a lower-pitched snort. Folks with a musical ear might be able to detect the tonal difference. The only way to test this is to listen to the snort, make your guess, then positively identify the animal that snorted. Keep careful records and you'll soon know how accurate you are.

But a better play is to avoid being detected—and "snorted to"—at all.

ANTLERS

In more ways than one, antlers truly are bones of contention. Scientists argue about why deer grow them. Hunters quarrel over how they should be measured. And many people complain that hunters attach way too much significance to them. Fanatics measure them, rank them and publish books listing their dimensions and relative status. They collect them, mold replicas of them, cast bronze statues of them, even name them (Hole in the Horn, Double Drop Tine). Clubs—some would describe them as cults—have been established to honor heavily antlered whitetails. Local "big buck" contests and regional conventions recognize the grandest racks of the year. Even casual antler admirers mount them on walls, carve them into art objects, incorporate them into belt buckles, knife handles, lamps and furniture. Aficionados hunt cast antlers in spring the way gourmands hunt mushrooms.

Okay, so some folks go a bit overboard. But whitetails themselves are the ones truly obsessed with antlers. Hey, we just admire the racks; they *grow* them. Some researchers claim that a buck expends as much energy manufacturing his rack as a doe expends producing and feeding a fawn. Now, investing time and alfalfa growing a fawn makes sense. It perpetuates the species. But antlers? Four months after they're completed, bucks cast them aside like last November's political posters. In a natural system where animals constantly compete for limited resources, this seems stunningly wasteful.

When you really stop and think about them, antlers aren't just wasteful; they're freaks of nature. Hey, those are naked bones protruding *outside* of an animal's body. Usually bones grow *inside* an animal as a support and frame to anchor muscles and assist motion. Some of them (marrow bones) manufacture blood cells. Antlers do none of these things. They are solid bone with no marrow; they anchor nothing, they support no muscle, they promote no motion. So what good are they? We'll get to that, but first let's investigate precisely what they are and how they are manufactured.

Opposite page: A dream buck! Humans aren't the only ones who admire bucks like this: so do does and other bucks. It's hard to believe that racks like this are shed and regrown every year. Below: The pronghorn is the only horned animal that sheds its horn sheaths every year.

BLOWING THE RIGHT HORN

As most hunters know, antlers are not horns, even though we sometimes casually refer to them as such. True horns are permanent head ornaments on cattle, sheep, antelope, bison and goats. They consist of keratin, the same protein in hooves and fingernails. Horns grow around a bony core from the inside out, enlarging as the animal ages. The only species that sheds its horns is the North American pronghorn, which also sports the world's only branched horn. Other species' horns are single-beamed, although that beam may be bent, curled and twisted into weird and wonderful shapes. Both sexes of horn-bearing

A dropped antler in North Dakota, reverting back to nature. Small rodents, insects and bacteria will recycle the nutrients.

species generally, but not always, grow horns; the male's often are larger or more elaborately shaped.

In contrast, antlers are solid bone and as deciduous as oak leaves, growing and falling annually. Not every deer species in the world produces them (Asian musk deer and Chinese water deer do not), but any creature that does is definitely some kind of deer; antlers are the exclusive badge and membership card of the deer clan. With two exceptions, they are also exclusive to male deer. The only female animals known to science that normally grow antlers are caribou and reindeer cows. The occasional antlered doe whitetail someone bags is rather like the bearded lady in the circus—just a bit overdosed on male hormones.

If you like your information short and sweet, the antler story is fairly simple. They sprout in early spring, grow beneath a velvet skin covering through July, and harden in August. In September bucks rub the velvet off, do a bit of sparring with their associates, then chase the girls through November, as late as January in the south. Mating finished, they ditch the antlers. The next March they start manufacturing their next set. Pretty basic stuff. But the details of this story, and the exceptions to it, are fascinating.

IN THE BEGINNING

Whitetails are born with *periosteum* tissue (fibrous connective tissue that covers bones) beneath their forehead skin just in front of their ears. The cells of this tissue are *antlerogenic*, which can be defined as follows: If you remember your Bible, you'll recognize Genesis, the beginning, in *-genic*. Add the prefix *antler* and you have the meaning — the "beginning of antlers" or "capable of generating antlers." And the emphasis is on "capable" because without the stimulation of a specific hormone, periosteum tissue doesn't do a darn thing. Does prance around with periosteum under their scalps all their lives and never grow antlers. So what is this magic elixir, this antler producing potion? Testosterone.

At about three months of age, buck fawns attain sufficient body weight to trigger the onset of puberty and antler production. This is the whitetail version of a boy's voice changing. The little buck's testes produce a small dose of testosterone which signals the periosteum to start laying down bone cells called *pedicles*, the familiar stumps atop a buck's head. These are the antler's permanent foundations. Each year pedicles grow larger in diameter so they can support the ever-larger structures growing atop them. This is why an old buck's antler bases remain thick and heavy even if he no longer has the vigor to produce equally massive tops.

The role testosterone plays in antler production should not be glossed over: It's essential. Castrate a buck fawn before his testes can begin producing testosterone and he will never grow antlers. But inject a female fawn with this natural drug—or an adult doe for that matter—and she will sprout bones atop her head. Injure the skin over these pedicle bones and antlers will grow.

ANTLERED DOES

Even in the wild, antlered does are more common than most hunters imagine. The highest ratio ever found was one antlered doe in every 900 does; the lowest, one in every 4,000. Most of these are spikes, but a few are small or medium-sized six- to eight-point racks.

Research shows that hormones are at the bottom of all this cross-gender dressing. Because ovaries naturally produce small doses of testosterone in addition to large quantities of estrogen (the female sex hormone), researchers suspect that during pregnancy some does might overproduce testosterone and initiate a short burst of one-time antler growth. Little velvet spikes usually result, and they remain permanently attached without further effect. The spiked females go on to produce normal fawns.

It is also possible, though not proven, that some infertile, antlered does suffered from their association with twin brothers while still fetuses. This happens in cattle and the infertile heifers are called freemartins. The placentas of still-developing fetuses fuse and the pair shares the same blood supply, permitting the male hormones that influence genitalia development to compromise the female's reproductive tract. This has been documented in European roe deer does, some of which go on to grow antlers, so it could happen in whitetails. The fact that antlered does are

KILLER DEER

Grizzlies are ornery and unpredictable enough to frighten people out of the woods, but whitetails can be just as deadly. Every now and then a rut-crazed buck will attack and gore a human. A half-dozen or more 10-inch tines wielded by 250 pounds of enraged beast are deadly weapons.

Usually such attacks are made by captive deer against their caretakers or photographers who foolishly get into the pen with them. Orphaned fawns hand-raised by compassionate country folk sometimes grow up to gore the hands that fed them—or any other person unlucky enough to come upon them during the rut. Similarly, park deer acclimated to tourists can metamorphose from corn-munching herbivores to frenzied killers. A single, agitated thrust of a buck's head can maim or kill.

To prevent such tragedies, treat all deer as wild, unpredictable animals. Expect the unexpected, especially during the rut. Your odds of being attacked are extremely slim, but if you wish to err on the side of safety, carry a firearm in the woods and fields during fall. Even a .22 rimfire handgun might save a life.

fairly common among whitetails, which often produce twins, and extremely rare among elk, which almost always throw single calves, supports this possibility.

Older does often suffer blocked or atrophied ovaries or adrenal gland tumors which may cause declines in estrogen production or increases in testosterone, leading to a variety of antler growth. If the doe produces enough testosterone, she may run through an entire annual antler cycle just like a buck, stripping velvet in early fall and shedding hardened antlers in winter as her hormone levels rise and fall.

Then there are nature's curve balls, those few does caught in the middle with both male and female sex organs. Depending on which organ dominates, these hermaphrodites may exhibit anything from velvet spikes to hardened racks. Whitetails with external female genitalia but internal testes instead of ovaries generally grow fairly substantial antlers because they produce testosterone instead of estrogen. Such deer, however, are not true females. They may, in fact, be freemartins or males in drag, so to speak.

TRANSPLANT FEVER

Periosteum is so effective at starting antler growth that if you cut some of it out and transplant it to a buck's leg, cheek or even ear, a pedicle will form there and an antler will grow. Such antlers aren't large, but they are shed and regrown season after season just like normal antlers. This explains why some "freak" bucks are found with third antlers growing beneath or between regular antlers.

Most likely, such bucks injured their periosteum or underlying pedicle in a fight and pushed a part of it to the unusual position. After the wound healed, antler growth began at the new site while continuing at the old site with its established pedicle. It's also possible that periosteum tissue was "misplaced" during development of the fetus, rather like a six-legged calf or two-headed snake. Even in nature, accidents do happen.

Finally, researchers have observed bucks sprouting supplemental antlers from forehead wounds beyond the pedicle sites. Apparently the injury served as a catalyst for velvet skin to begin growing.

The most intriguing documented antlered doe of all was an experimental animal from which a small patch of periosteum was cut away above the pedicle region without injection of testosterone, removal of ovaries or other de-feminizing tricks. And what do you suppose happened? She manufactured antler. This throws a monkey wrench into the works and implies that a wild doe could cut her forehead on a fence or the sharp end of a branch and give herself a lot more than a headache. Apparently female whitetails have a latent power to grow antlers, which could be activated by mere injury alone. As it turns out, wounding is critical to antler production in bucks, too, as we'll soon see.

VELVET BUCKS

Just as there are odd does, there are unusual bucks, too, and testosterone is the "smoking gun" behind most of them. The storied "velvet buck" of hunting lore is indeed a victim of castration, just as old hunters and cowboys have been claiming for centuries. Whether nipping coyotes or barbed wire fences administer the unkindest cut of all has not been proven. Tumors or disease probably account for loss of normal testicular function in the wild. Testes that fail to descend from the abdominal cavity can produce enough testosterone to initiate antler production but not enough to end it, leaving the poor buck with velvet antlers for life. Fortunately, the low doses of testosterone he produces do not drive him to use those antlers or pine for females. He's pretty much a sexual no-show.

If an unfortunate stag loses his testes in summer, he'll carry his velvet antlers forever as reminders of his "buckhood" cut short. The antlers do not, however, remain normal. Winter freezing kills the tips and sometimes all of the main beam. The frozen parts eventually rot and fall off in spring. But then the darn antler starts growing again. Often this cycle of partial dying and regrowth piles up fantastic collections of short points and bumps around the antler bases, giving rise to the famous "cactus" bucks.

Even more compact, amorphous growths have tumor-like appearances—big, ugly cones or blobs seemingly melting down over the buck's head. Where winters are mild, bases can enlarge to twice their normal size or numerous non-typical points will sprout. Racks do not, however, grow to record-book proportions, due to the inevitable accidental injuries of the growing tips and to a limited ability of the velvet antler to regenerate.

Repeated loss of the growing tips slows subsequent growth significantly. If experimentally cut off near the pedicle, however, a castrated buck's antler will regrow to its normal size. The pedicle is the birthplace of antler regeneration, rich in rapidly producing growth cells.

If a buck's gonads are excised in autumn while he has hard antlers, those bones will be shed within a week due to the sudden drop in testosterone. The next spring new antlers will sprout and grow normally, but they'll remain in velvet and never be shed. This indicates that once the initial shot of testosterone signals the periosteum to begin laying down the pedicle at puberty, something else triggers the start of each subsequent new antler growth. That something seems to be physical trauma or injury.

Testosterone production spurs the regrowth of antlers in spring. Antlers grow at an incredible rate—as much as a quarter-inch per day, faster than any other living animal tissue known.

HURTS SO GOOD

Various studies of captive bucks have indicated that after a buck's first antlers are shed, all subsequent antler production starts in response to the wounding of the pedicle, which bleeds slightly and quickly scabs over after the antler drops off. Velvet skin grows under the scab, pushes it off, and awaits the spring growth spurt. In experiments in which buck fawns were castrated after they'd produced pedicles but before they'd produced their first antlers, testosterone injections failed to produce antlers until the pedicles were surgically injured. Thereafter antler production began. Similarly, pen-raised does given testosterone injections produced pedicles, but didn't produce antlers until their pedicles were cut. If one was cut and the other left undisturbed, only the damaged pedicle would grow an antler. And in subsequent years the same side would again produce bone, but the uninjured side would not. Injury is essential for antler regrowth.

This fast-maturing young buck in his first autumn has grown "button antlers." Like an adult, he will shed these buttons during the winter, then start growing his first real set of antlers the following spring.

Antlerless bucks in the wild are sometimes called hummels. A mature hummel will display normal buck features and sexual behavior and will even father fawns, but will not grow antlers. This could be genetic, but probably relates to nutrition. In studies of red deer in Scotland, three sexually mature hummels were found to have small pedicles, so researchers injured one on each stag. Sure enough, the injured pedicles started growing antlers on two of the three animals. Thereafter those two deer progressed through the normal annual antler-growing and casting cycle, but only from their previously injured pedicles—disproving the genetic misfit theory. The one-antlered stags also sired male fawns that grew normal antlers, further proof that their genes weren't defective. The third test animal was found to have exceptionally small pedicles, suggesting it had been too malnourished as a fawn to grow a proper antler foundation. This study suggests that hummel whitetails, though rare, are probably victims of exceedingly poor nutrition. It pays to get a good start in life.

NUTRITION IS THE KEY

During a healthy buck fawn's first autumn, pedicles show as distinct bumps beneath whirls of hair on the forehead skin, earning the little guy the title of "button buck." Where nutrition is excellent, some precocious fawns show polished bone above the skin when they are only five months old. Believe it or not, at this time they can impregnate does, though in the wild this almost never happens because there are usually mature bucks around to do the job.

Most bucks produce their first visible, hard antlers when yearlings. These are

YOU GROW WHAT YOU EAT?

Maybe it's just coincidence, maybe it's proof of that old adage "you are what you eat," but antlers grow much like the plants that whitetails eat. And bighorn sheep horns grow like the plants they eat.

Bighorns feed mostly on grass which grows from its base up. This way it can tolerate being chewed off again and again, yet continue growing unabated. Similarly, a ram's horns grow from their bases upward, thus a ram can break off its horn tips (brooming) without stopping their growth. This is no small matter since horns are permanent structures critical to a ram's breeding status. If they grew from their tips, one false crash and somebody's rutting fun would be over.

Whitetails take another approach to life. Instead of blindly ripping off every blade of grass they pass over, deer select tender and nutritious forage, nipping a fresh shrub leaf here, a better one there. But shrubs and trees grow from their tips, much like whitetail antlers do, so excessive or repeated browsing can kill them. This is why whitetails can't live in large herds at high densities like bison and other grassland species can.

The fact that antlers grow from their tips explains many things—such as why they must be shed and regrown every year to replace damaged tines. And why they must be sheathed in sensitive, protective velvet while horns need not be. Snap off an antler's growth cap and you stunt or arrest its growth. This doesn't happen often in the wild, but every once in a while someone encounters a buck with one short, heavy stump antler that was obviously nipped in its formative stage. More often we see abbreviated, blunted tips, bent and crooked tines, even deformed main beams. Most injuries misalign or mash a growth cap rather than excise it entirely.

usually twin spikes or forks, but can be small six- or eight-point racks where soils are rich in minerals, plant nutrition is high and deer are in balance with their food supply. Recent research indicates that, contrary to popular belief, a buck's first and second racks are not a reflection of his genetic potential. Instead, these initial antlers reflect the health of the buck's mother. Healthy, well-fed does that give birth early, then provide superior milk, produce bucks with the largest first- and second-year antlers regardless of what the young bucks' sires had carried atop their heads. Only in the third year and later does the genetic inheritance from the father show, and then it does so mostly in increased mass rather than additional width or length of main beams and tines.

This calls into question the practice of culling spike yearlings in order to improve antler size in local herds. We really need to wait until a buck has completed his body growth at age 4 before judging his antler potential, for only when he's finished growing his skeleton and major muscles can he funnel maximum energy into antlers.

One study of spike bucks, however, clearly showed that where nutrition is good, yearling spikes can be genetically inferior to branch-antlered yearlings. In this study, spike yearlings went on to sire 44 percent spike offspring while branched yearlings fathered only 5 percent spike offspring. The problem with applying this knowledge in the wild is that hunters don't know whether the spike they are seeing is a genetic spike or a nutritional one. Given that in a reasonably balanced herd, mature males with large racks will do almost all of the breeding, hunters would be wise to let spikes pass if they're trying to get some bigger bucks in their area, or if they don't need venison immediately. These deer are probably just late-born and will catch up with the rest of the boys in later years.

In one famous study, average antler size in an experimental herd of deer from mediocre genetic stock *doubled* in three generations when all the deer were fed a high-protein/high-energy diet. This probably means that the herd had been poorly nourished for years and required several generations on superior forage before genes were finally able to reach their true potential. Or, perhaps, consistently high nutrition over several generations somehow improved the genes themselves. Either way, nutrition is the key. Without it even the best genetics are suppressed.

IT'S NOT NICE TO FOOL MOTHER NATURE

How do we know photoperiodism signals antler growth? Through experiments.

To test the timing connection between a deer's pineal gland and antler production, scientists removed the tiny gland from a test subject. That buck managed to grow normal antlers, but way off schedule. He started late and during the fall rut he was still in velvet, proving that the tiny pineal gland located in the brain is indeed the alarm clock of antler production.

In other experiments with photoperiodism, researchers held bucks under controlled lighting conditions. By speeding up natural light/dark sequences, they induced bucks to grow and shed three sets of antlers in 12 months. If light/dark cycles were held evenly at 12 hours each per day, bucks that entered the experiment with hard antlers retained those bones for as many as four years. But if test subjects had been kept outdoors in natural light beyond the winter solstice, then pulled into the 12 hour light/12 hour dark experiment, they went on to shed their old antlers and grow new ones normally, but they held onto their new antlers for years.

If bucks were kept under constant light, or 8 hours of light and 16 hours of dark or vice versa, they grew, hardened and cast antlers, but not at normal seasons. They might grow in the fall and cast in the spring, for instance. This experiment indicated that, in addition to the pineal gland that starts the sequence based on changing day length, whitetails have some sort of inner clock that governs some of their annual life cycles. In humans we call these biorhythms or inner clocks.

In other experiments, photoperiodism was overwhelmed by the antler injury response. If one of a buck's pedicles was amputated in late summer, it would regrow immediately, leaving the buck with one hard antler and one velvet antler. This indicates that the rapidly growing cells of the antler bud are more critical to initiating growth than is photoperiodism. Once the growth cells are stimulated, they'll grow regardless of light levels and seasonal duration. In nature, of course, it would be extremely rare for a buck to break off a pedicle in late summer, but if you ever run across a half-and-half buck, you'll know why.

TIMING IS EVERYTHING

The timing of annual antler production is a product of *photoperiodism*, life's little sundial that wakes up all sorts of natural phenomena like bird migration, pelt shedding and hibernation. In early spring, increasing daylight strikes a buck's retina, stimulating it to send an electrical signal to the pineal gland, which converts the news to a chemical message and relays it to the pituitary gland. It's a long and winding road. The pituitary, essential for regulating body growth, is nestled deep within the brain. When it finally gets the spring message, it secretes hormones into the blood, and when these reach the pedicles, *voila!* Antlers start growing, usually between mid-March and late April in the North, as late as May in Florida.

TOUCHY FEELY

Budding antlers don't start out as naked bone, but as a matrix of cartilage blanketed under fuzzy velvet skin bulging up from the pedicles. Velvet, a modified extension of the skin and hair surrounding the pedicle, is tough but sensitive. Because of the longitudinal direction of its thick layer of collagen fibers, this special skin will tear lengthwise but is extremely difficult to rip in cross section. Some 6,000 tiny hairs per square inch of velvet surface protrude like a phalanx of spears to ward off insects. Each sprouts from a sebaceous gland that secretes a tiny bit of oil which may have some repellent properties. The oil also makes the antlers slightly slippery and more resistant to abrasion.

More importantly, each velvet hair is anchored to a nerve fiber which, like a cat's whisker, "feels" objects. You might say each rising antler is its own radar tower

Antlers start growing between mid-March and late April in the north, and as late as May in Florida. In the early stages of development, antlers are quite soft and easily damaged. Like all bucks, this fellow is steering clear of thickets where he could hurt the tender, growing antler tissue.

signaling within fractions of an inch how close its ever-lengthening tines are to trunks and branches. This early warning system prevents accidental damage. Even after the velvet is dead and gone, bucks remember the spatial dimensions so well that they can stretch back to scratch an itch with the tip of a tine or wend their way through a thicket without bumping a branch.

CONSTRUCTION UNDER WAY

Swelling antlers are about 80 percent protein and 20 percent ash (mostly calcium and phosphorus with a mix of trace minerals including manganese, iron, bismuth, silicon, titanium and even a touch of gold). Superficial temporal arteries above each of the buck's eyes extend up to the pedicle and branch into about a dozen main shipping channels, carrying fuel to what will be, for roughly 100 days, some of the fastest growing bone tissue known. During peak growth in June and July, whitetail tines lengthen a quarter-inch per day, a rate exceeded only by antlers of larger deer like moose (three-quarters of an inch per day!). Such production requires more minerals than deer can ingest with their normal diets, so the animals literally steal it from their rib bones and make up the shortfall once antler growth has stopped. This is an example of beneficial osteoporosis. Tests with radioactive mineral traces have shown that antler minerals are first deposited in the body skeleton before being resorbed and redeposited into the antlers. Unfortunately, they cannot be stockpiled.

During peak antler mineralization, resorption of rib bone calcium and phosphorus may approach 25 percent. Here again we see the importance of nutrition to the overall health of whitetails. With abundant, high-quality forage, bucks expend minimal energy piling on maximum body weight, leaving plenty of excess protein to funnel into giant antlers. Interestingly, winter starvation has not been shown to decrease subsequent antler size. One group of bucks kept on half-rations for five weeks and another group for 10 weeks during early spring grew just as much antler as did a control group on a full diet when all three groups were given complete, nutritious diets June through September. The antlers of the 10-week group were slightly lower in bone density, but tine number and length were not reduced.

In a similar study, bucks put on a restricted diet from January through April lost 30 percent of their pre-rut weight. In May they were allowed free access to complete rations and—you guessed it—they grew normal-sized antlers.

These studies prove at least three things: 1. The critical antler growth period is June through August; 2. Summer nutrition plays the key role in this growth; and 3. Winter feeding has little bearing on antler production, which helps

explain how those far north Canada bucks can grow such huge racks. Better quality summer forage is the main reason bucks in Midwest corn country are so much bigger and heavier than bucks their age in deep South pine woods or on granite-soil, mature conifer forests. Summer foods in these latter two environments may not have as much protein content or be as readily available as are many farm crops, second-growth shrubs and trees bordering fields and waterways. Summer droughts in any region without irrigated crops probably translate into smaller antlers, too, since forage quantity and quality suffer.

Antler size and good nutrition go hand in hand. To grow large antlers, bucks need adequate food to satisfy their body requirements as well as antler growth. No matter how good the genetics, you won't find big bucks where food and nutrition are in short supply, or where the deer don't live long enough.

HOT BLOODED

It takes a lot of blood to supply the raw materials for growing antlers, so it's not surprising that a second arterial system flows through the pedicle into the middle of the cartilage matrix. A third roadway pulses blood within the velvet skin, nourishing it and its extensive network of nerves. So much blood flows through velvet antlers that they register 104°F on their surface, the same as a deer's core body temperature. The arteries are especially thick and elastic so that they can contract abruptly and shut off blood flow within seconds in case of injury. You can see the tracks of these arteries as channels molded into the surface of hardened antlers.

The obvious cooling effect of so much hot antler surface exposed to the air has inspired some scientists to speculate whether antlers evolved for thermoregulation, functioning like the huge ears of desert jackrabbits or the panting tongues of dogs.

During hot summer months, velvet antlers may serve a buck as thermoregulators, helping to keep him cool. This is a fringe benefit of the antler-building process.

Since antlers are grown in summer when cooling is needed, then die and are ditched for the cold seasons, this idea makes a certain amount of sense.

But the hypothesis weakens as soon as we remember that only males produce antlers. If getting rid of excess body heat via antlers were essential, wouldn't does grow them too? And Canadian bucks would have smaller antlers than Florida's Key deer, not larger. Of course, antlers as radiators on males could be a secondary adaptation of convenience. If deer were evolving ever larger and more elaborate racks for defense or sexual display anyway, why not throw in the air conditioning? Well, the best we can do is speculate; we may never know for sure. Nonetheless, velvet antlers do help summer bucks stay cool. Call it a fringe benefit.

TIP-TOP SHAPE

While it seems natural to think of an antler as pushing up from its base like a blade of grass, it actually grows out from its top. Like a mason laying down layers of brick, a "growth cap" of special cells at the tip of the antler lays down collagen protein cells that then form into the various tissues of the growing antler. Near the tip the cells are largely undifferentiated, the rough equivalent of raw mortar. Farther down, older cells begin to form longitudinal collagen fibers shot through with tiny blood vessels spilling down from the growth cap. This is the forming cartilage, sort of like uncured bricks. Below this cartilage is the spongiosa which is calcified cartilage, a spongy-looking, soft bone honeycombed with blood vessels draining down through the pedicle. Spongiosa (consider it nearly cured brick) makes up the bulk of the growing antler, solid enough to hold the superstructure's shape but soft enough to bend or break from impact damage. So, despite the bulging, fragile appearance of velvet antlers, they aren't like water-filled balloons. Perhaps an inch of the growing tip is truly fragile, rather more like gelatin than liquid. The rest is fairly solid and durable.

SCIENTIFIC CURIOSITIES

The rapidly replicating cells of a velvet antler tip look and behave suspiciously like cancer. In fact, they are high in some of the materials present in bone cancer. Despite this, antlers are the only animal tissue that does not become cancerous. Some scientists have credited this to the fact that antlers live only a few short months, not long enough for cancer to get started. But the permanent velvet antlers of castrated bucks live for years and these antlers have never been found to be cancerous either. So, predictably, antlers are of interest to cancer researchers.

Because antlers fall off and are regenerated every year, scientists also study them for insights into limb regeneration. Among mammals, deer are the only family that can regenerate a lost appendage. Many worms and amphibians, some lizards, and some crabs and insects can regrow limbs, but practically no mammals can. Even though antlers aren't functioning limbs like arms or toes, they may reveal some secrets that could unlock regeneration of those critical body parts.

HOW DID ANTLERS EVER GET STARTED?

No matter how much we learn about antlers, one puzzle may always remain: How did such bizarre bones ever evolve? We can only scratch our heads, study the extensive fossil record and hypothesize.

Fossilized skulls from dozens of extinct ungulates around the world display bony head ornaments of amazing variety. Comparing these to the skulls of living beasts enables scientists to place the deceased within various mammalian orders, families and often genera and species. An extinct group of Protoceratids specialized in spike and forked horns atop their noses as well as their heads. Mounted on a den wall, their skulls would stimulate considerable conversation.

In North America various pronghorns grew long spiraling horns, flat-topped ramming horns and four, five and six horns sprouting from as many points on the creatures' skulls.

Among these primitive ungulates were numerous Giraffids sporting bony ossicones (skin- and hair-covered protuberances like those possessed by today's giraffes). Most of these were larger and more elaborate than the stubs giraffes wear today; some were even

multibranched. What if these were used for jousting? Could repeated butting, prying and poking have skinned and broken them? And could these beasts have developed some method of repair, something like a bone spur that often follows injury even in humans? Maybe a gene similar to the ones that direct limb regeneration in lizard tails was at work. The upshot would have been that Giraffids that could not only heal their ossicones but toughen them, even enlarge them, would have subsequently won more battles, sired more calves and passed on their genes.

The odd-looking muntjac of Asia, one of our most primitive deer, carries long, permanent skin- and hair-covered pedicles that look remarkably like giraffe ossicones, except that short spike antlers grow from the ends of them. The unique velvet stage of whitetail antlers looks suspiciously similar to ossicones, too, and the mandatory wounding for regeneration of antlers seems to echo the healing of an ancient, battered, skin-covered bone, doesn't it? Hmmm. Things that at first glance appear so different may in reality be not so far apart when you get down to the core of the matter.

THE SHAPE OF THINGS TO COME

It is often possible to identify a mature buck from one year to the next by the shape of his antlers: Size, shape configuration and tine-placement are usually similar from year to year. Some bucks also have distinctive face and chest markings that help in identification.

Miraculous as its role in generating new tissue is, an antler's growth cap might also play a critical part in controlling an antler's classic shape. Researchers suspect that instead of a single growth cap there may be several tiny growth points spaced strategically atop the pedicle. As new antler begins swelling, these growth point cells are carried upward, gradually diverging according to their initial spacing from the others. Each tip eventually starts a new tine rising from the main beam.

It is also possible that individual tine growth points are somehow generated along the growing main beam, which would help explain those fantastic non-typical antlers. Velvet hairs are generated on the growing tips, and that is unusual. Most mammal skin cannot generate new hair once the underlying follicle is lost. So if the growth cap can initiate hair, why not tines?

Scientists also point to the possibility that the arteries supplying the growing antlers might have something to do with their shape. CAT scans have shown that in red deer, at least, a single artery supplies the spike antler, but in branch-antlered stags this single artery branches along the pedicle before rising up to fuel the antler, each branch serving a different tine. The terminal fork of the antler was served by a single artery, but it branched before the tine did, each branch running into one tine. Researchers wonder: Must arteries branch before antlers can? And do they somehow give rise to the antler's shape?

Next is the possibility of nerves directing antler conformation. Researchers have noted that if a buck injures its pedicle, grossly non-typical antlers will erupt, but when a buck is sedated before its pedicle is injured, normal antlers grow. This implies that the deer must feel the pain before it can respond with unusual antler growth. The younger the antler and the closer the injury to the pedicle, the greater the non-typical growth. Supporting this "nerve stimulation" theory is the fact that a buck that injures its pedicle while conscious will usually grow similar atypical antlers for three or four years in a row without further trauma to the antler or pedicle. The implication is that somehow it remembers the injury.

Nerves are so critical to antler growth that once a buck has produced its first pedicle, nerves alone will stimulate subsequent antler production. In experiments, pedicles and even surrounding forehead bone were excised from bucks, yet nerves "remembered" the previous antlers and initiated a second set from the forehead wound site. And while periosteum and pedicles transplanted to noses, leg bones and other sites did grow antlers, they never assumed the traditional whitetail configuration. Only when transplanted into an area supplied by the nerve that normally serves the growing antler was traditional antler shape generated.

Clearly we still have a lot to learn about antler growth. Someone with a scalpel and microscope had better get busy.

MATURATION & DEATH

As soft, new cartilage is laid down and the growth cap is pushed ever upward, old cartilage begins to gradually mineralize and harden from the base up. Eventually this shuts off most of the blood vessel system growing from the pedicle, leaving the antler tops to be serviced primarily by the external arteries, which may be part of the reason antlers gradually but consistently taper ever smaller toward their tips. As antlers mature in late July, mineralization increases through August. The core remains somewhat spongy and retains some blood flow, but salts build up in the remaining arteries, clogging and hardening them. Essentially, over the course of several weeks, both antlers and their

The earliest stage of drying and stripping of the velvet. Notice how the tip of the velvet is starting to split. In the next day or two the buck will completely strip the velvet from the now-hardened antlers. Generally, prime-age bucks in good health are the first to complete the velvet removal process.

velvet are choked to death by a form of hardening of the arteries. This seems to be brought about by ever-rising testosterone as the season progresses and decreasing daylight again signals the pituitary to do its thing. By late August or early September in the North, as late as early October in some parts of the South, antlers harden and their surfaces toughen. Like all bone, they are mostly calcium and phosphorus. They are also dead and bucks are itching to use them.

SHARPENING THE WEAPONS

Generations of hunters have been told that bucks rub velvet from their antlers to relieve the itching. But how much itching can they feel if the tissue is dead? Since we can't feel what bucks feel, we don't know that there is absolutely no itching sensation, but evidence suggests there is none.

Researchers once severed the nerves leading to a buck's antlers just prior to velvet shedding—and he rubbed the temporary skin off anyway, right on schedule. In other experiments bucks were injected with extra testosterone while their antlers were still in the growth phase and highly sensitive. They tackled shrubbery head-on and scraped the velvet off anyway, bleeding profusely.

Velvet stripping, then, is a behavioral response to rising testosterone levels. It's questionable if bucks even realize they are removing a layer of anything. Once they begin antler-rubbing, they continue all through autumn until testosterone levels finally fall in December or January.

Serious hunters know that velvet stripping is not the same as rub marking, which comes later in fall. When stripping velvet, bucks thrash small, flexible saplings and shrubs. Later they'll rub larger, less yielding trunks. They may work aggressively and clean their new antlers in an hour. Sometimes they'll work at it for a few minutes at a time over the course of a day or two. Old, sickly or young bucks often take even longer, sometimes weeks. Distracting strips of velvet hanging from beams are often eaten. Usually they're left dangling from brush.

When a new antler is freshly stripped it is lightly stained with blood, but this is soon washed or worn off, leaving the tines white until repeated encounters with a variety of limbs and trunks stains them dark. Evidence of this is the darker tone of many antler bases where the rough pearling abrades and traps more sap and stain while smoother tines often remain whiter.

As a rule, the largest, healthiest, most heavily antlered males strip their velvet first; the puny, weak, spindly antlered bucks last—more evidence that testosterone is at work. These large-antlered bucks are also more aggressive, more active and usually more belligerent. They carry themselves with an air of confidence, even superiority, for they are the "top dogs" in the neighborhood. Their physical condition determines their social ranking and predicts their breeding success during the rut. Thus a buck's mission in life is to grow the biggest rack of antlers he can, for his genetic future depends on it.

Opposite page: When stripping off velvet, a buck thrashes small, flexible saplings and shrubs. When finished, he may even pull the velvet from the branches and eat it plus any shreds left hanging near his eyes and mouth.

Younger bucks often keep their antlers longer than older, more mature bucks. This buck has just recently lost an antler: Note the newly formed scab.

GETTING RID OF DEAD WOOD

Because they are supercharged with testosterone, the most nutritionally fit bucks rut hard, take on all comers and quickly wear themselves out. As a consequence their body condition suffers; they may lose as much as 25 percent of their pre-rut weight. When they get too run-down, their testosterone levels crash. Almost overnight they visibly shrink in stature and influence, retire to a quiet corner, and within a week or two dump their once essential antlers without a backward glance. Meanwhile younger, smaller bucks, still with some fat on their bones, maintain their testosterone levels longer and cling to their racks several more weeks. This is when they often get a chance to breed an old doe missed during her first estrus or an extra-healthy fawn reaching her first estrus.

A buck's antlers quickly go from "solidly attached" to "breaking off." Bucks have been seen fighting vigorously one day, then casting their racks a week later. Researchers have wrestled bucks to the ground by their antlers, then seen them fall off at the pull of gravity a few days later. The casting process begins when falling testosterone levels permit a layer of cells to absorb calcium at the juncture of the pedicle and antler. A thin layer of the once-solid bone is soon full of tiny holes and chambers as if eaten away by acid. Like melting spring ice, the remaining walls give way under the antler's weight. Surprisingly, usually a bit of blood flow can be found at the pedicle, suggesting some tissue was still alive. Probably this is just a rupturing of the external walls of the blood vessels within the pedicle, which are waiting to feed the next antler. A scab forms, and beneath it the surrounding skin grows outward to create the new velvet cap, tiny hairs all erect, awaiting the spring. This is essentially a bud or blastema, which is different from a scar.

That's another unique quality of antlers. Somehow velvet skin redirects the collagen it manufactures into an orderly formation as opposed to the disorderly collagen formation that causes scar tissue at other injury sites. It's magic.

The pedicle scab is essential to antler regrowth. If full thickness skin grafts are carefully sewn over the pedicle before a scab can form, no new antlers will form. Normal bucks require the injury of dropping their old antlers before they can generate new antlers; no one knows exactly why, but scientists suspect it has to do with how antlers evolved millions of years ago (see page 105).

BLUEPRINTS FOR SYMMETRY

We know what antlers are and how they grow, but what makes them assume that traditional whitetail shape? And what makes them get big? Or non-typical?

The traditional whitetail form is species-specific—no other deer has antlers quite like it, though the Sitka blacktail of the coasts of Alaska and western Canada does come close. Certainly each whitetail displays subtle, minor differences in form—for instance, one buck's main beams may flare far to the side while another's curve in—

but the basic format remains constant across the species: the main beam rises and angles slightly to the side of the head, then curves forward, often turning in considerably near the tips. From this main beam, vertical tines arise, a substantial brow tine usually beginning an inch or two from the base. Then there is usually a gap of several inches before additional vertical tines arise, as many as six spaced evenly along the remaining length of beam. This shape is a genetic inheritance firmly fixed in the whitetail's DNA and passed down for centuries. But how did it get started in the first place?

As good an explanation as any is that paired antlers evolved as fighting weapons, specifically grappling tools to enable one buck to solidly grasp the antlers of another and wrestle him to the ground while keeping the antagonist's deadly tines at bay. Thus the entire whitetail rack is shaped like a grasping tool, a basket of "fingers" that lean or curve in slightly to grasp an opponent's tines. The spacing between tines provides numerous catch points to prevent an opponent's rack from slipping too far forward or backward, ensuring a relatively tight fit. This provides maximum grip for serious pushing, pulling and twisting—which is the whitetail buck's fighting technique. The brow tine might, in theory, provide the last line of defense against serious eye and face punctures, though the number of one-eyed bucks photographers see each fall suggests this may be wishful thinking at best.

Alternatively, the brow tine could be viewed as a vestigial spike from the whitetail's distant past. Like the spike antlers atop today's more primitive deer of the tropics, it might have been used for deadly territorial defense against interloping members of the same species—a stabbing spear instead of grappling hooks. Where resources are scarce, as in deeply shadowed tropical jungles where most vegetation grows high overhead, deer must defend feeding grounds. But in temperate regions,

Antlers evolved primarily for fighting other males of the same species. The shape provides for maximum grip when engaged in pushing, shoving and twisting matches. Interestingly, antlers can also prevent fights (a lesser buck will often back off). And big antlers may attract does waiting to breed.

What God Hath Joined Together

Although a whitetail's rack is superbly designed for engaging his competitor and protecting himself, it isn't foolproof. Under the force of two 250-pound brutes crashing together, racks often spring slightly apart, then snap back, locking opponents in a death grip. Every year a few hunters and game wardens come upon antler-locked bucks.

Sometimes the duelists can be separated by sawing one antler off. More often one is already dead, the other nearly so. In the most bizarre situations, one buck is found alive bearing just the head of his antagonist, coyotes having eaten the rest of the dead buck right under the nose of the frightened survivor.

Though it's extremely rare, out on the Plains where whitetails and mule deer intermingle, bucks of both species have been found antler-locked in tragic interspecies struggles.

where lush summer forage provides an excess of food, deer can tolerate more territorial infringement: share and share alike; there's plenty to go around.

But come mating season, a limited number of females might be worth fighting over. And in those battles the buck with a few more protective antler tines might survive while the spike-adorned battlers impale one another to death. Thus, any temperate deer that happened to grow freak antlers with excess points would have survived longer and passed his extra-tine genes to more generations, thus starting the trend that has led to today's spectacular racks. This is just speculation.

Another viable theory is that, in addition to grasping and blocking opponent's tines, antlers evolved ever larger and more elaborate to impress and discourage fighting altogether. Brandish an obviously superior weapon and the competition backs down. We'll further explore this idea later in this chapter (see pages 117 and 122).

Bucks are like gluttons at a smorgasbord. Since they live in temperate zones where abundant summer sunshine produces more vegetation than they need for body maintenance, why not convert it into fancy antlers? Bone instead of meat.

But we still haven't explained the antler's classic shape. A famous wildlife scientist once hypothesized that all deer antlers are molded at least in part by their environment. Thus a whitetail's rack curves forward instead of stretching far to the sides so that it doesn't get caught between tree trunks. And its plow-like shape allows it to push through the brush whitetails usually live in. In contrast, a tundra moose's big palms stretch wide apart because it seldom frequents forests; its antlers are slanted to spill off big winds. Those ideas make a certain amount of sense, but how do you account for caribou? The vertical palmation of their racks would slip a headwind, but a right angle breeze would sure put a lean on them. And all those tines would be a nuisance in the woods. Of course, the largest racked caribou subspecies live on the treeless tundra, the smallest racked in the forests. So maybe there is something to this idea.

The classic whitetail antler conformation could also be a simple, random product of evolution. For whatever reason, the early whitetail began developing multiple tines in more or less today's standard style, he and his offspring survived and passed on that gene. That other shapes were tried is evident by the unusual racks we see today: drop tines, forked tines, non-typical racks. As always, Nature tosses out the occasional oddball just to see what happens. If she gets lucky, the new model succeeds; if not, it fades out. So far the classic whitetail antler shape seems to be a winner.

Large antlers signify a superior buck, a buck that will do the bulk of the breeding in his territory if he has maintained dominance and won battles with other bucks. This is all attractive to females. Thus, he will pass his genes on to future generations.

THE KEYS TO BIG ANTLERS

Regardless of what influences antler shape, we do know what influences size: nutrition, maturity, genetics and mineral supply, in roughly that order. Before any buck can grow a large, symmetrical rack, he must be fully mature, completely healthy and have plenty of nutritious forage. Having a father with a heavy rack helps, too, though heredity is a less significant factor. That's because poor genetic quality is pretty much self-limiting. If large antlers signify a superior buck, help him dominate lesser bucks, and make him attractive to the females, he's going to do the bulk of the breeding in that neighborhood and pass on those genes. His sons and grandsons will perpetuate the pattern. Meanwhile, mature bucks within that same population that are genetically programmed to grow puny antlers just aren't likely to sire enough fawns to make much of a difference.

The exception to this occurs when superior bucks are harvested excessively over a long period while puny bucks are left to breed. Shoot every 8- and 10-point in the herd every fall, ignore the short, narrow, spindly beamed, mature 6-points and you could throw a monkey wrench into the works. The key word here is "mature." Usually when buck harvest is too high in any area, as it has been for decades in some eastern and southern states, all genetic classes of bucks are killed long before they mature. No one really has an accurate picture of their genetic potential because most of them get shot when they're 1½ years old. A buck isn't fully mature until he's at least 3½ or 4½. Up until then his body is still growing, and a growing body precludes maximum antler growth.

Because antlers are "luxury organs," meaning they aren't essential for survival, they are last in line at the dinner table, so to speak. Only when a buck has finished growing his body skeleton and muscle can he afford to pour energy into antler production. Again, that happens after age 4 or so. Peak antler growth occurs between ages 5 and 8, after which most bucks begin to decline. Therefore maximum antler production is a product first of maturity.

Antler growth is also a product of nutrition, which includes trace minerals.

THE LIMITS TO GROWTH

Since superior nutrition is known to increase antler size over generations, shouldn't it be possible to breed and feed a line of "superdeer" to produce ever larger and larger antlers? Probably not.

A careful study of the world's deer suggests that there may be a limit to antler size in each species. The bigger the deer, the larger its antlers in proportion to its body, more or less. Thus, tiny deer like pudu, brockets and roe deer grow tiny spikes or at most three-point antlers. Mid-sized deer like sika deer, mule deer and whitetails grow mid-sized racks. Big deer like elk, caribou and moose grow the largest antlers of all.

These massive racks are not just matching the larger body size of the animals growing them. They are proportionately bigger. The caribou produces the largest rack per pound of body of any deer.

Scientists have noted that pedicle size relates to antler size. That is, the larger in diameter the pedicle, the heavier the antler, suggesting that increasing pedicle size on whitetails could lead to larger antlers. But even if this were possible, the whitetail's skull size limits pedicle size. Also, since antler minerals are largely taken from the body skeleton, skeletal size probably puts the brakes on antler growth: We wouldn't expect a buck with 4 pounds of rib bone to produce 20 pounds of antler.

A good rule in the natural world is "never say never," but in the case of whitetail antler production, don't expect anyone to discover a 300-inch typical rack anytime soon.

Sometimes superior nutrition can enable a 3-year-old buck to grow bigger antlers than a 5-year-old on poorer forage. And that same 3-year-old would grow even bigger antlers when 4 years old, and even bigger when 5, 6 and 7. So age and nutrition work hand in hand. The older and fatter the buck, the more impressive his rack.

Minerals, although often discussed and fretted over by hunters, are rarely the missing link in antler growth. A growing antler consists mostly of protein. Only after the protein frame has been laid down are minerals needed to harden it. Mineral deficiencies might have more to do with antler strength than maximum size. The antlers from old bucks have been found to be less dense than those from younger bucks, either because the racks were too large to be fully mineralized by available bone calcium or because the higher doses of testosterone generated by the older bucks hurried antler maturation and velvet stripping before mineralization was complete. Since bucks pull minerals for antler hardening from their skeletons, they should have plenty for the job even in deficient soils. They have considerable time during their "off-season" to replenish supplies gradually. This said, there remains a largely unexplored connection between forage protein, carbohydrates, minerals and vitamins. It may be that slight mineral deficiencies interact with vitamins or some other factors to reduce antler growth via inefficient transport of nutrients or incomplete metabolism.

There is a lot we don't know. But we do know that optimum antlers result from optimum age, nutrition and minerals.

Age, nutrition and minerals result in optimum antler size. Of these factors, age and nutrition may be most important.

Overall health also plays a strong supporting role in maximizing antler size. Obviously no diseased buck, no buck with a broken leg or infected wound, can take full advantage of the nutrition available to him. Thus his body growth, fat production and antler size suffer. Aside from injury, good health is usually a result of good nutrition. A well-fed deer is less likely to fall prey to viruses, bacteria and diseases.

Some studies of penned red deer have shown a positive correlation between social rank and antler size. That is, the buck at the top of the pecking order could grow larger antlers as a result of his high status. If his antlers were broken in battle or cut off by researchers, not only would his status fall that rutting season, but the following year he would grow smaller antlers and remain lower on the totem pole.

Whether such social ranking influences whitetail antler growth in the wild is highly speculative. Wild whitetail bucks, even though they often live in small bachelor groups, are not forced to live cheek-to-jowl in pens the way those red deer were. Nevertheless, whitetails do establish a rough pecking order each fall based at least partly on antler size, body size and individual aggression.

In general, bucks with small antlers learn through sparring not to mess with bucks with bigger antlers, but sometimes a slightly smaller-racked buck with a larger body and/or a more aggressive nature calls out a bigger-racked buck and soundly beats him. Whether this results in the winner growing larger antlers and the loser growing smaller antlers the following year remains to be discovered.

What researchers have established is that social stress can lead to decreased antler production. When populations are dense and small bucks frequently bump into larger, older bucks, the small bucks manufacture smaller antlers. This may be due to inhibited testosterone production. So many big, ornery old-timers patrolling the neighborhood somehow act as a psychological lid suppressing secondary sexual expression in younger animals. Where populations are sparse, each buck is free to act out his fantasies, imagine himself the king of his hill, puff up on testosterone and grow the largest rack local nutrition allows. This may be another reason bucks in some sparsely populated farm areas reach trophy proportions so regularly.

That leaves genetics. All else being equal—health, maturity, nutrition—the buck with the best genetic profile for large antlers will indeed manufacture the biggest rack. It's just that simple. Remember, though, that excellent nutrition over several generations can produce bucks with antlers far superior to their genetic inheritance. This may be similar to the phenomenon of high school basketball players, both male and female, who seem to get taller with each new generation. Consistently great nutrition across generations either enables genes to fully express their potential or somehow improves those genes. Either way, it's exciting news because land managers usually have many opportunities to improve forage quality.

FREAKS

What about the huge non-typicals—the drop-tine bucks, the bent and crooked tines? A variety of accidents and mysteries can account for them. Most deformed antlers result from injuries while in velvet. Because the velvet skin is so tough, the

Opposite page: A buck with unusually high but typical antlers. Judging from the broken brow tine, this buck has been an active participant in the breeding season.

Drop-tine buck. The reasons for non-typical racks are many ... sometimes it's injury and sometimes it's heredity. Similar deformities can repeat year after year.

arteries so quick to control bleeding, and the growth so fast and determined, bent and broken tines usually heal and often continue to grow; they usually complete the hardening process as well. Broken tines that hang from the main beam by enough velvet to maintain blood flow eventually mature into drop tines. But not all drop tines result from this. Some are genetically induced and can be traced through several generations. Antlers that show a drop tine or other odd point in the same position year after year suggest—but don't prove— a genetic basis.

Experiments have shown that freak tines can be initiated by injury and then repeated in subsequent years' antlers. Cutting a velvet antler sometimes, but not always, induces a tine, bump or other abnormality to sprout at the wound site. As discussed earlier, a buck fully conscious at the time of injury can apparently "remember" it and grow a similar deformity on the following year's antler. This abnormality may persist into the third and fourth antlers, but may decrease in prominence.

Gamekeepers in England apparently observed this phenomenon long ago for they used to "pepper" a stag's velvet antlers with bird shot to induce non-typical growth. The earlier in the antler growing cycle the injury occurs, the greater the unusual growth. Researchers who have tried to induce such abnormal points by injuring anesthetized bucks generally failed, which suggests the nervous system is part of the process.

In experiments with captive deer, antler buds just beginning spring growth were cut and wedged open to create bizarre antlers with numerous basal beams and odd points, suggesting that at least some impressive non-typical antlers could have started when a wild buck ran headlong into a tree, fence or other stationary object. It does not, however, prove that this is the only cause of non-typical racks. Genetics probably enters into the equation as often as not, even though non-typical bucks do not automatically sire non-typical offspring. What role the mother plays in determining non-typical antler growth is not known, but it must be substantial since one non-typical buck-doe mating can produce a normally antlered offspring, yet that same buck bred to another doe might produce an outstanding non-typical buck. Data regarding non-typical antlers is muddy and inconclusive, proving once again that although we've learned a lot about whitetails in the past few decades, they remain quite mysterious.

One peculiarity often noticed among wild deer is a deformed and usually weak antler opposite an injury. For instance, a buck with a broken right rear leg might grow a poor left antler. This "contralateral response" supposedly compensates for imbalance in the buck's body. Some observers have noted that injuries to front limbs resulted in deformed antlers on the same side of the body, but in other cases front limb injuries resulted in no antler deformities, so the process is far from cut-and-dried. One theory is that a buck favoring one leg due to injury is more apt to

Small cheater points can appear one year and disappear the next. On a young buck like this (notice the lack of fighting scars on his face and ears), the cheater may be an indicator that this fellow will grow more non-typical antlers in upcoming years.

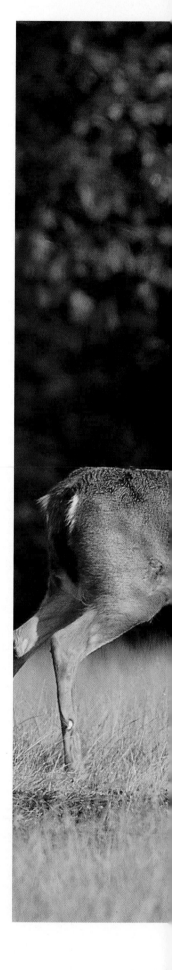

accidentally injure velvet antlers, though experiments have not borne this out. Even when bucks with amputated legs did not injure their antlers, the side opposite the injury was stunted in size. Some scientists suspect that effects from the leg injury are crossing in the spinal cord and stimulating a nerve serving the opposite antler. The jury is still out on this hypothesis.

SO, WHAT ARE THEY GOOD FOR?

Now that we know what antlers are and how they are grown, let's explore their many known and possible uses.

WEAPONS OF DEFENSE

Multi-tined antlers make such obvious weapons that folks automatically assume they are designed to fend off wolves, cougars and other predators. Bucks certainly use antlers for defense, but that isn't their primary purpose. If it were, does would sport antlers, too; after all, they have fawns to protect. And, if antlers were strictly defensive weapons, why would bucks throw them away in winter when they are weak and vulnerable due to cold and snow?

Faced with these facts, we scratch our heads until we dislodge the next most obvious answer: Since only bucks have them, antlers must be designed for fighting over females. Autumn is the whitetail breeding season, and that's when we see bucks antler to antler, pushing and shoving. Since only males carry antlers and they begin developing them at puberty, they are obviously secondary sexual characteristics, like beards on men.

Yes, that must be it. Bucks grow antlers in spring and summer, harden them in early fall, hone them and practice using them on shrubs and trees, then clash their way to victory at the peak of the rut. Breeding concluded, they drop the dead weight and rest easy through the hard winter. Perfect.

Well, not quite. Certainly bucks brandish their antlers for jousting, but they could accomplish the same thing without them, as every nonantlered animal does. Male cottontails settle breeding disputes by chasing and kicking one another. Horses bite, rear and flail with their hooves. Wild turkeys jump, flap and kick at each other with their sharp spurs. Pheasant cocks cackle and flail at one another. Clearly, combatants do not need antlers to settle their differences, and they certainly don't need elaborate antlers. Roe deer in Europe sport rather puny 4- to 6-point racks rarely more than 8 inches long, yet they manage to settle their differences and win female favors during the rut.

If fighting determined who got lucky each fall, then strength and body bulk would long ago have taken precedence over fancy antlers. Bucks that funneled extra energy into growing muscle and bone would have won more fights, bred more does and passed on their genes for large size. But instead of bigger whitetails, we have bigger antlers. For some reason large antlers have been selected over bigger body size. So the question remains: Why all those long, pretty tines atop North American whitetails?

RED BADGE OF STATUS

Bucks with large antlers flaunt their headwear in front of subordinates. Here the bucks are still socializing in their bachelor group, but the biggest buck is making a scrape to proclaim his dominance within the territory.

Most humans agree that a tall, wide, symmetrical rack of antlers is a whitetail buck's crowning glory. Deer think so too. So conscious are they of antlers that one buck can back another down simply by displaying his head gear. And if a mighty-racked buck breaks off an antler in a fight, he may be immediately challenged and often routed by lesser bucks. Males that have lost antlers while fighting have been seen to slink away, becoming shy and reclusive. Some drop out of the rut altogether. Is it possible, then, that antlers grow big and elaborate not *for* fighting but to *prevent* fighting?

Does also notice antlers. Though researchers haven't conclusive proof, they suspect females are selecting large-antlered bucks to sire their fawns when given a choice. This partially explains why we often see does running through woods and fields hours before their estrus, attracting and trailing a line of antlered suitors. While the boys chase her and battle one another, she gets a good look at the merchandise. The fact that does rarely run off to breed small-antlered bucks while bigger

ones are fighting supports this theory. Instead, they refuse the younger male's advances and await Mr. Macho. When a hunter bumps a mating pair of whitetails from an isolated thicket, the buck is usually the largest he's seen in that area.

To some degree, then, antlers are badges of maturity and status symbols, the gold Rolexes and red sports cars of the whitetail world. If they've got it, they flaunt it, and flaunting circumvents quite a bit of dangerous fighting. He who has the biggest rack rarely has to bloody his nose to prove his superiority. We see this anytime a significantly larger-antlered buck walks in on a smaller buck and a doe. The little guy takes one look and gets the heck out of Dodge.

Still, growing such elaborate displays for bluffing and advertisement seems like overkill. If cardinals can defend territories and attract mates just by wearing bright red feathers and singing, why do whitetails need all those bones? Wouldn't it be more efficient just to grow a red nose or something?

This buck's big antlers can serve as status symbols, advertising his dominance to all the does around. These does may be more likely to breed with him because of his striking crown of antlers.

SUBSTITUTE FAWNS

This brings us to yet another possible explanation for antlers: *the surrogate fawn theory*. This is a beautiful combination of scientific research and deductive reasoning that drives to the heart of this question.

Here's how it works: Since antlers are seasonal and too poorly distributed (only bucks have them) to be effective weapons against predators, unnecessary for body cooling, excessively elaborate to be mere jousting tools, and poor substitutes for bulk and strength to win by intimidation, they must play another, less obvious role. But what? Behavioral biologists suggest this idea: What if antlers were a buck's way of proving his overall genetic superiority, his survival fitness? What if they represented

Older, mature bucks make good guardians for does during the rut. By keeping young, aggressive males at bay, mature bucks enable does to rest without frequent harassment.

genuine proof of suitability for siring a female's fawns, proof that they would benefit the entire species?

This makes sense when we consider the role genetics plays in survival of the fittest. The only way fitness can be passed to future generations is for parents to be tested before breeding. Ranchers do this with cattle by selecting bulls that have shown superior weight gain, hardiness, muscularity or other desired genetic traits. They pair them with disease-resistant cows that gain weight rapidly and calve easily. This information is gleaned by marking each animal, weighing and measuring it and keeping accurate records throughout its life. But in the wild, what mechanism can help determine the most fit breeders?

Whitetail does are tested simply by the fact that they live long enough to produce fawns. Females that are alert enough to avoid high-speed Fords and toothy coyotes, strong enough to survive the winter and healthy enough to produce fawns pass on their genes. The longer they live and the more fawns they successfully raise, the more their superior genes influence subsequent generations. But the doe is only half the genetic equation. What tests bucks for the same survival abilities?

The answer, of course, is antlers. Analyses of antlers reveal that the minerals in them equal those produced in the milk of lactating females. Because antlers require about as much time, raw materials and energy to grow as do fawns, they might very well function as surrogate fawns, proving that the buck who grew them does indeed have the kind of superior survival genes needed to produce hardy offspring. Before a buck can grow his biggest antlers, he must live more than four years. This proves

he's adept at staying out of trouble, avoiding predators, finding enough food and surviving lean times. Next he must be capable of finding the best forage because the more protein, calories and minerals he ingests, the larger his antlers. Then he must be metabolically efficient at converting those raw materials into a superfluous body appendage, just as a doe must be efficient at producing a fawn. Such a superior buck must also be strong because, even with his big rack, he'll probably bump into one or two other bucks with nearly equally impressive antlers, and they'll insist on wrestling to settle breeding rights. Finally, he'll have to be fast to keep up with the doe as she romps through her territory, trailing a train of panting suitors.

Bingo! Super stud. Just the sort any doe would love to have father her next batch of twins. He'll throw female fawns with all the traits they'll need for optimizing their own ability to produce fawns, and that will propel the species onward. Antlers, then, are like big neon signs proclaiming *Grade A Certified Hunk. Pick Me.*

THE WHITETAIL'S SWISS ARMY KNIFE

Essentially, antlers are the whitetail equivalent of a Swiss Army knife—versatile, do-it-all tools. They're more than adequate for fending off wolves in a corner, great for scratching itches and fine for cooling the hot summer blood. They impress the neighbors and avert a lot of painful, exhausting, needless fighting. But if push comes to shove, a thick, wide, tall rack helps its bearer resist the tines of his rival. Finally, antlers prove a buck's genetic fitness and help him woo fertile does so that he can pass those superior genes to as many future generations as possible.

This page: Whether they're fighting tools or doe attractants, antlers (note the unusual double beam here) are strikingly dramatic. Next two pages: Two good bucks spar to see who outranks whom in the breeding pecking order.

CHAPTER THREE

BEHAVIOR
&
SEASONS

THE SPRING FLING

Spring brings a mixed blessing to whitetails. Sprouting plants provide a lifesaving abundance of concentrated protein, vitamins, minerals and carbohydrates. But increasing daylight signals the pituitary gland to stimulate production of adrenal and thyroid gland hormones. The effect is like giving a shot of gas to an idling car engine. The deer's metabolic rate shoots up and suddenly it needs a lot more fuel to keep going. At the same time it must replace lost body tissue and, in the North and West, migrate back to its summer range. As if that weren't enough, in May the major fetus and antler growth periods begin. Finally, in late May in the North, late June to early July in parts of the South, the does must isolate themselves, defend territories and drop their fawns.

Opposite page: This young, spotted fawn seems to be all legs. Fawns at this age are never far from escape cover and no longer depend on just camouflage and lack of scent to escape predation. They are now quick and speedy, and have a good understanding of their territory, compliments of their mother.

131

DYING TO STAY HOME

It was long assumed that reducing whitetail overpopulations in localized areas, such as parks and upscale suburbs, required killing does over a wide area; otherwise new deer would quickly move in to fill the empty habitat. But recent research suggests this is not the case. By identifying, targeting and completely removing matriarchal clans from small areas, researchers were able to clear those areas of deer for years. Nearby clans were so faithful to their traditional home ranges that they did not move into the vacant spots.

Killing only part of a territorial matriarchal clan does not accomplish long-term population control because survivors, faithful to their traditional haunts, soon refill them with fawns. The key is to remove the entire clan.

THE RETURN HOME

In the mild climate of the Deep South, whitetails live on their small home ranges year-round. In the North they often must migrate to small wintering yards. The spring melt frees them from this seasonal limitation. Usually between late March and mid-April they begin migrating back to traditional summer ranges. Both sexes are notoriously faithful to their traditional haunts. Once a fawn has been led from its first summer range to its winter yard and back again to summer haunts, it will remember that route for the rest of its life. If a fawn's mother has died over the winter and the little deer hasn't socialized sufficiently with other members of its matriarchal clan—aunts, cousins, grandmothers and great grandmothers—it might not be able to retrace its migration route back. Then it is forced to wander and becomes more susceptible to predation and accidents. Other matriarchal groups will not welcome unrelated orphaned does to their territories. Thus it must find unoccupied habitat—unlikely in most places— or live on the edges between established clans. Yearlings of both sexes usually form wandering bands that roam these no man's lands, trying to find a place to fit in.

Such forced wandering helps whitetails find and fill new habitats but also puts the wanderer in jeopardy. Because the best of everything has been taken, the deer must now live on poorer quality

A doe and last year's fawns migrating away from their winter yard. Youngsters learn the routes to the yard and back to summer range from their mother. Although a bit of snow remains, spring is on its way.

forage. Without the protection and guidance of older does, it becomes an easier target for predators. And while it meanders through strange country, getting chased and harassed, it is more likely to become a road-kill statistic.

BACHELOR BASICS

Orphaned yearling bucks also wander, but eventually they latch onto other bucks and join bachelor society, usually in late summer or early fall. Exactly how this works isn't known. Normally a doe, about to give birth, physically kicks and chases her older fawns away. Both male and female fawns will return a month or two later and be accepted back into the family home range, but by late summer or early autumn the little buck, showing its first antlers, is driven out. Aggressive does rebuff the yearling male wherever he roams. Constant harassment by does might also be the reason bucks live and forage in slightly poorer quality habitat during spring and summer.

Anyone who thinks bucks voluntarily surrender the best forage so that the "women and children" have a better chance for survival has been watching too many Disney movies; deer are neither chivalrous nor altruistic. It is extremely doubtful that bucks even realize they're eating slightly lower quality food, let alone making a conscious decision to do it for the good of the herd. Instead they just go where it's peaceful. As described in the digestive system section of chapter two (pages 74–81), bucks are equipped physically to handle greater quantities of lesser quality forage. Perhaps it's no coincidence that this works hand in hand with harassment by does to foster the formation of bachelor societies on the fringes of doe territories.

Throughout most of the year, bucks hang out in bachelor groups. It's only during the rut that these cliques break up and buddies become enemies. By winter, the group is often back together again.

LEARNING THE ROUTES

Why would a buck whitetail migrate through miles of suitable summer habitat to reach a specific, distant home range? And why pass several suitable wintering areas to reach the same old spot he's always used? In a word, tradition.

Migration routes are learned. A fawn learns its first summer range from its mother, who then leads the impressionable youngster to its first winter range. But before its second summer, rarely its third, a buck is kicked out of Mom's territory. Left to wander, often over dozens of miles, it meets up with other bucks and follows them to new summer range. This is significant because it moves young bucks far from their mothers, sisters and cousins, reducing inbreeding. Bucks that don't find male companionship in places where populations are low often end up pioneering completely new territory.

Come late autumn, most bucks remember that first wintering area Mom introduced them to and head back to it, ignoring equally good sites en route. They spend winters with their mothers and sisters, but it's doubtful they even recognize them.

MIGRATION GYRATIONS

Buck or doe, young or old, some whitetails may migrate as many as 100 miles back to their summer territories, depending on local conditions. In Idaho they've been recorded crossing several major mountain ridges and a river valley or two—ignoring thousands of acres of suitable summer habitat in the process—in order to reach their traditional summer ranges. In the northern reaches of the Great Lakes states they've been known to go more than 40 miles. Even on the Plains they might trek more than 30 miles. Of course, many whitetails live their lives on practically the same few acres. There's no place like home.

Migrations may proceed in fits and stops with inclement weather or deep snow holding things up for days. Spring snows might even force deer back into their deep winter yards. Under ideal conditions they might dash all the way home in one night. During migration, both sexes intermingle freely, forage together and don't worry about whether they're trespassing on the others' territories. But a month or two later, they'll be segregated and the females will fiercely defend their individual fawning grounds.

SOMETHING TO FAWN OVER

By mid-April a pregnant doe is spending most of her time eating. For the previous four months her fetus barely developed, reaching just two pounds after 130 days. Within the remaining 60 to 80 days of her pregnancy the fetus or fetuses (usually one the first time, then two or more in later pregnancies) will quickly balloon to 5 to 8 pounds depending on subspecies and nutrition of the doe. This delayed growth strategy enables does to pull through lean winters yet still produce healthy fawns by utilizing the flush of spring growth. Scrawny and stillborn fawns indicate poor spring forage, most likely due to overpopulation. Rarely, malnourished does spontaneously abort or reabsorb the fetus. In most cases fawns weighing less than 4 pounds do not survive.

A week or two before she is ready to deliver, a doe begins defending a personal fawning territory of 10 to 40 acres, probably by scent-marking the boundaries. This is the only time of the year in which any whitetail is truly territorial and any doe is antisocial. Within a month or two of giving birth, the female will relax her territorial defense and begin associating with her female relatives again. She'll also allow her previous years' fawns back to feed and bed with her.

The benefits of defending individual fawning territories are numerous. First, this spreads deer across the landscape, increasing available forage for all. Second, it decreases the odds that predators will find an easy concentration of helpless fawns. Third, it prevents fawns from following the wrong doe and getting lost or abandoned. Finally, it controls population by limiting available fawning sites. When whitetail densities reach 100 per square mile, even in the best habitats there is no room for more nurseries. Excess does are forced to drop their fawns in the poorest habitat where they are easily found and devoured by predators. Even if they aren't eaten, they are often abandoned to starve. Young mothers simply can't behave normally under the stress of being chased from other does' territories again and again, never finding a quiet place of their own.

During this territorial phase, bucks live in corridors between fawning grounds. Young bucks, especially, walk on eggshells so as not to incur the wrath of an expectant or new mom. It's a good time to lay low if you're a male of the species.

Predictably the oldest, most experienced does, which are also usually the highest-ranking in any clan, get the best fawning territories. Because offspring inherit some of their mother's social standing, they often assume ownership of her territory when she passes to that big alfalfa field in the sky. Young, low-ranking does are forced to use poor quality, fringe habitats which they must share with or try to defend from groups of displaced yearlings or bachelor bucks—another reason young does are less successful at raising youngsters to adulthood.

THE STORK ARRIVES

For all their vigilance in protecting their solitude, does are rather nonchalant about where they actually drop their spring packages. Only in places where predation is routinely high do they gradually learn to seek out dense cover and sometimes even

Shortly before she gives birth, a doe will defend a personal fawning area, the older and more experienced females claiming the best habitat. Because fawns will bond with just about any large creature for a few days after birth, the mother must defend her area against other does, her own yearlings and bucks.

Left: A doe grooms her new fawn. A clean fawn means little scent for predators to detect. Above: Newborn fawns will approach and imprint on any large body that happens to be in the area—including the photographer! How many times have we heard of people adopting so called "orphans," when in all likelihood the mother was quite close by.

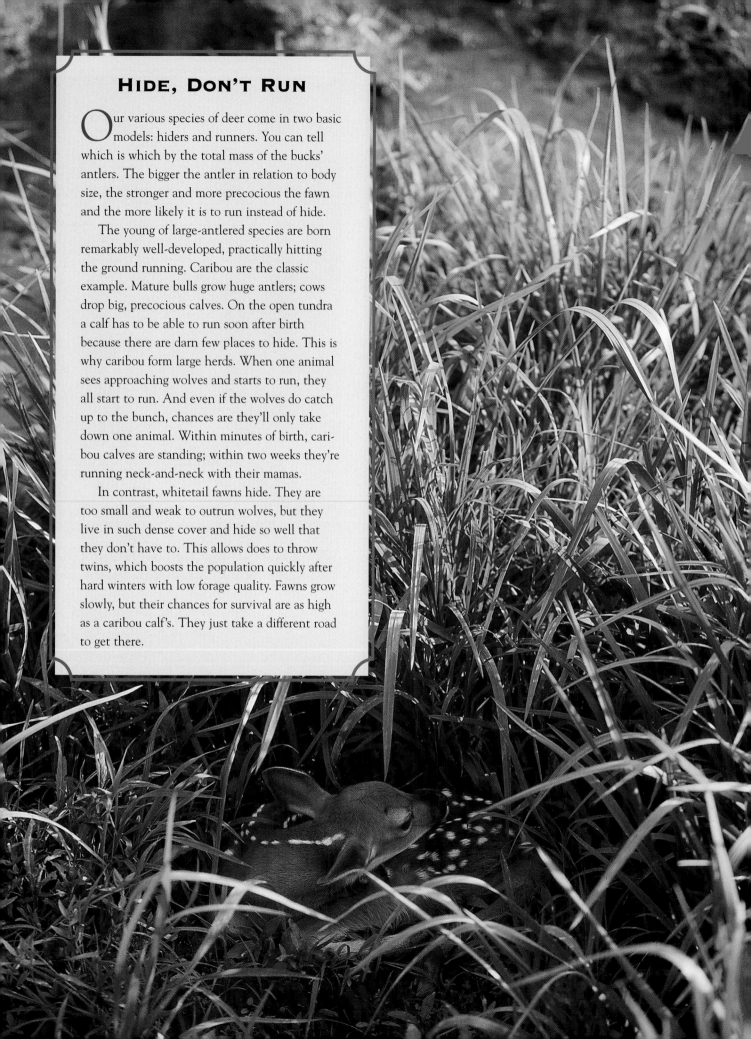

HIDE, DON'T RUN

Our various species of deer come in two basic models: hiders and runners. You can tell which is which by the total mass of the bucks' antlers. The bigger the antler in relation to body size, the stronger and more precocious the fawn and the more likely it is to run instead of hide.

The young of large-antlered species are born remarkably well-developed, practically hitting the ground running. Caribou are the classic example. Mature bulls grow huge antlers; cows drop big, precocious calves. On the open tundra a calf has to be able to run soon after birth because there are darn few places to hide. This is why caribou form large herds. When one animal sees approaching wolves and starts to run, they all start to run. And even if the wolves do catch up to the bunch, chances are they'll only take down one animal. Within minutes of birth, caribou calves are standing; within two weeks they're running neck-and-neck with their mamas.

In contrast, whitetail fawns hide. They are too small and weak to outrun wolves, but they live in such dense cover and hide so well that they don't have to. This allows does to throw twins, which boosts the population quickly after hard winters with low forage quality. Fawns grow slowly, but their chances for survival are as high as a caribou calf's. They just take a different road to get there.

small islands. Otherwise they stand or lie nearly any-where, from grass to open woods, while the fawns emerge front-feet-first, then head and shoulders.

The actual labor may last from a half hour to several hours. Twins emerge about 20 minutes apart and begin nursing within 10 or 15 minutes, often while the doe is lying down. If she does not lie down, her fawns will rise on shaky legs within about 20 minutes to nurse. They'll even follow her a hundred yards or so when just a few hours old. She generally leads them a distance from the birth site to reduce chances that predators will find them. She also thoroughly cleans the area, eating all afterbirth and any vegetation it touched. Of course, she licks each fawn again and again, cleaning and drying it while learn-ing its scent and beginning the bonding process. Because the world is new to them, fawns foolishly trust any large, animated object that does not eat them. This is why they so readily bond with humans who find them and take them home under the misapprehension they've been orphaned. Normally two or three days under the quiet, uninterrupted care of Mom sends them on their way to becoming truly wild, furtive creatures.

FAWN 54 WHERE ARE YOU?

Given the curious nature of fawns, we might wonder why more of them don't wander off to be lost forever. It turns out their dams "train" them to stay home. When a doe leads her fawns to new bedding sites after each feeding, she keeps them within her exclusive fawning territory. Being faithful by nature to the places they know, even little whitetails confine their strolls to a limited area. Only later, when they are strong enough to outrun predators, will Mom lead them into her wider world. Meanwhile, she can easily find them within her small 10- to 40-acre fawning territory.

AFTERNOON OF A FAWN

The routine in the first two or three weeks of a spotted fawn's life is pretty simple. Nurse, follow Mom a short distance into fresh bedding cover, lie down and watch the world go by. Because fawns hide with their heads stretched out flat or tucked back against their sides when people stumble upon them, we tend to think this is their normal posture. It's not. Like adult deer they spend most of their waking time head up, ears cocked, paying attention—the stance of any self-respecting prey species. Only when something approaches do they assume the hiding position, and that is a much more elaborate production than meets the eye.

By attaching heart monitors to fawns, researchers have discovered that fawns will go into suspended animation when predators approach. The reaction resembles that of an opossum "playing dead." When undisturbed, a resting fawn's heart beats about 178 times per minute, and the fawn breathes about 20 times per minute. But when approached by a human researcher, a monitored fawn would drop its head, lay back its ears, and either stretch out or curl into as tiny a package as possible. Amazingly, a fawn's heart rate would plummet to just 60 thumps per minute. More than half the time the fawn stopped breathing altogether. If the biologist sat quietly nearby, the fawn's heart rate and breathing slowly returned to normal. But if the "predator" moved suddenly, the little test subject's heart rate and breathing in-stantly dropped again, though not quite as low as the first time. And when the researcher walked away, breathing and heart rates quickly returned to normal.

Opposite page: A young fawn hiding. Researchers have found that fawns will go into suspended animation —a form of playing dead—when predators approach.

This doe will visit her fawn five or six times each day for feeding and grooming. Then she will go away and leave it to bed alone—a great strategy for keeping predators from finding the youngster.

Here is physiological evidence to explain why fawns are such successful hiders. It isn't just their spotted coat and nerves of steel. Their little bodies actually shut down, preventing them from bolting. There is little or no breathing noise, no breath to smell, almost no heartbeats to hear. And since the fawn's scent glands haven't fired up yet, there is virtually no odor.

Does protect their hiding fawns by separating twins by as much as 80 yards, moving them up to 300 yards after each feeding, and staying away herself so as not to draw attention to the site. She'll watch diligently from a distance and charge in to attack a predator or run around it in a whitetail's version of the broken-wing routine. Her ploy is to distract and lure trouble away from her fawns. The older and more experienced the doe, the greater her fawns' chances for survival. In studies, young does lost three to four times more fawns than did older does. Old does moved their fawns farther between bedding sites and were more likely to charge predators.

Merely smelling coyote urine in the vicinity of her fawns would prompt an experienced doe to move them to a different area, usually into denser cover. Fawns in poor cover are much more susceptible to coyote predation because these wild canines hunt primarily by sight. In parts of the Southwest they've been documented finding and eating more than 80 percent of the spring fawn crop. In prime habitat, fawn losses to coyotes rarely exceed 30 percent.

Does return to nurse their newborns four to 10 minutes at a time, 5 to 6 times each day. Fawns consume 4 ounces during each of their first few sessions, and drink 8 or 9 ounces per feeding by their third or fourth week, by which time they are nursing only three or four times in 24 hours—often only at night where disturbance is high.

The first milk is thick colostrum which provides disease antibodies. Fat content ranges from 10 to 18 percent, twice that of dairy cow milk. Whitetail milk is also considerably higher in energy and protein. It is among the richest milk known in the mammal world! On this nutrition-filled drink fawns double their birth weight in 10 to 14 days.

As the fawn matures, it not only grows stronger but also wilder. By day seven it is as likely to run from a human as lie still. If it runs, it will probably win the race. It also begins to follow its mother, who sometimes must nudge it down with her head or foot to make it stay.

By its third week, a fawn is beginning to nibble vegetation. After week five its digestive system is functioning well enough that the little deer can survive without milk, but it continues to nurse whenever it can until nearly five months old—although some are weaned as early as 10 weeks. If food is scarce, a doe's milk quantity will decline, but butterfat content will increase to make up some of the difference.

Even newborn fawns may rise to stretch several times each day. They usually walk a short distance before bedding again. Does find them by memory or by sniffing for their faint odor: probably the scent of her own grooming saliva, possibly odor from the fawn's interdigital glands. A doe licks her fawn's anal area vigorously while it's nursing to stimulate a bowel movement. Then she eats the excrement to remove all odors. If a fawn has moved too far for the doe to locate, she'll call it with a soft mewing. The fawn then leaps up and runs to Mamma. Because she cannot recognize her offspring from another doe's by sight or sound, she may briefly find herself feeding the wrong fawn. Mom notices the difference by smell alone. Then she usually walks away from the interloper. Sometimes, however, she will adopt an orphan.

TEXAS TOGETHERNESS

Evidence that habitat shapes behavior can be seen in open-country whitetails. In some parts of Texas does have been found foraging together in open grasslands with their fawns hidden nearby. They do not defend individual fawning territories as do northern deer, probably because food is evenly available over grassland habitat. The Texas deer probably find safety in numbers too. All does will respond to bawling fawns, so any mother grazing nearby increases any fawn's chances when coyotes come snooping.

MORE BUCKS FOR YOUR BANG

Roughly 53 out of every 100 whitetail fawns born is a buck. This is to compensate for the increased mortality rate of male youngsters. Because of their more

Fawns Out of Synch

Even though the majority of Northern fawns are born in a short spring period, a few are born well outside of "normal" dates. Births have been recorded in every month of the year. In the tropics this is standard practice because there is no distinct seasonal abundance of forage, but why would a doe in New England have her fawn in, say, August? She probably didn't conceive during her first estrus. Within about 28 days she would have recycled to try again. If this second estrus also failed, she'd be ready in another 28 days, and this January conception would result in an August birth.

While it might seem wasteful of nature to even try pulling such a late-born fawn through winter (the fragile little thing would still be in spots when the snow started falling) there is an adaptive benefit. In the unusual case of a sudden climate change, extremely late- or early-born fawns might have a survival advantage, enabling the species to adapt quickly and continue to thrive. Nature likes to keep her options open.

aggressive, inquisitive natures (not to mention the stupefying effects of testosterone when that hormone kicks in), buck fawns get into trouble more regularly than their sisters. They are more likely to wander off on their own, investigate strange sounds and odors, fall into pits and pools, get entangled in wire, and attract the attention of predatory felines, canines and hungry eagles. Even if he survives his fawn year, he is more likely to die from fighting during the rut.

For some reason well-fed does on highly nutritious, underpopulated range produce more female than male fawns, enabling the herd to expand quickly. Undernourished does on low-quality range throw more bucks. This is seen as nature's attempt to reduce populations. The way it works is unknown but might relate to hormone production as a result of diet or stress. Does that conceive late in their estrus cycle also tend to throw more males than females, which works out well since late-estrus breeding generally indicates a shortage of bucks.

All Together Now

It's no coincidence that the majority of does in any region drop their fawns within a few days of one another. Survival of the fittest has programmed that phenomenon for two reasons.

First, fawns that are born when forage is abundant have a greater chance for survival than fawns born when vegetation is dried up or frozen off. Over the centuries, fawns born too early or too late died. Those born on the proper schedule passed on this genetic predisposition until the trait was firmly bred into the species. Thus, most Northern fawns hit the ground during late May or early June. Coues' deer in the Southwest key their fawning to the summer mountain rains when forage is most abundant. Fawns in parts of the Deep South don't arrive until July, probably because the milder fall and winter climate places fewer demands on them. Since there is no seasonal abundance or scarcity of tropical forage, whitetails in Central America have their fawns at any time of year.

The second advantage to concentrated birthing is "swamping" predators, the theory being that most of the youngsters will grow large enough to escape while wolves and cougars are contentedly digesting the first few they catch. Dribbling fawns out over the summer would merely provide a constant supply of easy predator meals. Though swamping works well for many herding ungulates on the open plains, its usefulness among whitetails has been questioned. Tropical whitetails

survive quite handily with a year-round fawning season. Swamping may be of limited effectiveness among non-herding deer distributed evenly in heavy cover.

MALE SOCIETY

During the burst of spring birthing, male whitetails more or less hide out, keeping to the relatively safe corridors between individual fawning territories. As a general rule the more open the habitat, the larger the bachelor bands: more eyes, ears and noses to detect danger. In most places two or three bucks hang together. While it seems they have nothing to do, in reality they are hard at work building antlers. As noted in the section on antlers in chapter two (pages 93–125), this requires about as much energy as producing a fetus and is nearly as important. A big rack means breeding success and the genetic advancement of the species. So the boys eat, rest and eat some more, rebuilding their winter-wasted bodies and pumping protein to their rapidly growing antlers.

Bucks are remarkably tolerant and social during this period, going so far as to occasionally groom one another. When one rises to feed, his buddies soon follow. Where one goes to bed, the others go too. They are a social unit, finding comfort in numbers and rarely fighting because they've been chemically emasculated. Since the end of the rut their testosterone levels have hovered at annual lows, a fact that keeps the peace. If bucks were saddled with autumn testosterone doses, they'd be at each other's throats, er, racks, and chaos would ensue. Growing antlers are fragile and wholly unsuited to fighting in June. So bucks get along, now and then rearing to kick at one another to maintain the pecking order, but never knocking heads.

While not quite as exciting to hunters as autumn, spring is a busy season for whitetails, a crucial period in the struggle for survival.

Building antlers requires as much energy as growing a fetus. The plan? Become an eating machine, all summer.

IN THE GOOD OLD SUMMERTIME

Just because it's the lazy days of summer, don't think whitetails have it easy. Sure, food is abundant and temperatures are mild, but deer still have to avoid predators, raise fawns and put up with bloodsucking flies, ticks and sundry internal parasites. Still, compared to winter, summer is a fat season. As plants mature and become less nutritious, deer keep nosing out the latest mast and fruit crops: apples, grapes, cabbages, acorns, chestnuts, pears, mushrooms, rose hips, corn, wheat, oats, beans. When drought hits they zone in on watered lawns, irrigated crops and lush alfalfa fields. Any fresh, new growth is eagerly attacked.

During wet years whitetails get adequate moisture from their forage, but they still drink where water is available. Real trouble starts when heat and drought shrink water supplies, forcing deer to drink daily, stay near water and come in contact with a virus-carrying midge that infects them with deadly epizootic hemorrhagic disease (EHD), or blue tongue. Some researchers believe blue tongue and EHD are the same disease caused by variations of the same virus, others think they are distinct diseases. Either way, the affliction is almost always fatal. After the biting midge transfers the virus into a deer's bloodstream, the microscopic agents multiply and interfere with the vascular system's blood-clotting mechanism. Within a few days the infected deer bleeds to death internally, its tongue turning blue with hemorrhage. The first EHD outbreak was diagnosed in New Jersey in 1955. Since then it has plagued many parts of the country, but is particularly bad in the Plains states. Fortunately, herds quickly bounce back to fill vacant habitat. Mule deer and pronghorns are not as vulnerable as whitetails to EHD, but they also die from it.

Whitetails also suffer from anthrax, tuberculosis, salmonellosis, lumpy jaw and other bacterial and viral diseases that cause local die-offs. Then there are lung worms, brain worms, liver flukes and viral infections of the skin that produce warts or papillomas. Botflies lay eggs that hatch into larvae that crawl through and feed upon mucous in the nostrils. Lice live and feed on the skin. Ticks have attached themselves to fawns in such numbers that they've killed the poor youngsters or made them blind. While some rare diseases like anthrax ravage entire populations, most afflictions and most parasites don't kill whitetails unless they are undernourished and weak. Again, this is Nature's way of trimming overpopulation to keep a species healthy.

GROWING UP

Opposite page: A whitetail emerges from a northern conifer forest to feed on pond vegetation.

After their "infant" stage, roughly the first month of life, fawns become more active and enter the equivalent of their childhood. By two weeks they are fleeing predators instead of "playing dead." After 18 to 32 days twins begin bedding together and initiating their own activities instead of awaiting directions from Mom. When she's around to watch for trouble, they cut capers, run, chase and generally have a good

Young deer learn social skills from adults and then try them out on each other. Here two Wyoming fawns show aggressive body posturing over a food source.

time. This is their brief period of irresponsible play in a lifetime of caution and struggle, so they make the most of it. As they grow, the dam's territorial aggression wanes and she gradually extends her range and re-associates with her female kin, sometimes forming matriarchal family groups. While the old does forage, young cousins romp and get to know one another.

What looks like simple play among fawns is really essential training in survival skills and establishment of a pecking order. The young deer are developing muscles, learning to leap and dash, honing reaction times, and preparing for the hard tasks of competition and survival. The biggest and most aggressive youngsters dominate the smaller and more hesitant. Fawns learn by watching their elders, so offspring of dominant (older) does quickly learn how to be aggressive and establish dominance over the young of lower-ranking (younger) does. Also, fawns of older does are generally healthier and larger than fawns of young does, so they have a size and strength advantage. The biggest and best get bigger and better, and that drives the species forward.

Because of their increased activity, this is the time when weak or malformed fawns fall prey to predators. Now they are visible, leave a scent, and stick out like sore thumbs to experienced predators. Where once there was a handful of ornery does and lots of dense brush, now there are spotted fawns leaping and bouncing everywhere. Fawns that aren't fast, careful or obedient enough become one with the coyotes and bobcats, black bears and roaming dogs. As always, nature winnows her crop ruthlessly. She has no space for inferior specimens. Weather, disease and predators are not getting any weaker; neither can whitetails.

RETURN OF THE YEARLING

When does no longer defend their small fawning territories, their yearlings from the previous spring are welcomed back to the fold. Does that have lost newborn fawns almost immediately reclaim their older fawns. Until these reunions, yearlings live in small associations (gangs) of their own age group on the fringes of fawning zones, trying their best to stay away from those ornery new mothers. It's a difficult, rather dangerous period for the "teenagers." They no longer enjoy the benefits of association with older, wiser deer so are more likely to wander into trouble. Predators catch them, cars hit them, fences entrap them. Inexperienced, they do dumb things—rather like human teens.

Twins usually stay together near the only summer home range they've ever known, and if they stay long enough, they eventually rejoin Mom and meet their new siblings. Thus do yearling does begin their lifelong association with the local clan. Not so the bucks. If they haven't already wandered away, they rejoin Mom for just a short reunion. Within 2 or 3 months testosterone will turn them into intolerable pests, constantly disturbing females as they try to rest and feed. None of the females are ready for mating, so they—especially the alpha female—chase, kick and flail at the youngster until he takes the hint and hits the road. *Good-bye, Mom! Good-bye, Sis! I'm off to see the world.*

Rejected by the fairer sex, too immature to join the men's club, the poor yearling buck wanders and wanders, sometimes 20 miles in a night, looking for love in all the wrong places. Often he'll hook up with other unwanted yearlings far from home and find some solace. It's a sad odyssey, but one with a purpose. This forced

A yearling buck in an aggressive stance protects his feeding area. Young deer always seem to be in the wrong place and are constantly forced to be on the move or trying to defend their little piece of turf. That is what happens when you're low in the pecking order!

emigration is another of nature's ways of mixing the gene pool, reducing inbreeding and making sure any new genetic wonders are disbursed far and wide.

MATRIARCHAL TERRITORIES

With temporary fawning territories abandoned, family clans are free to roam their entire summer range. Within this area might live grandma, two or three grand-daughters, maybe even three or four great-granddaughters. A doe can live to 20 and still be fertile in her teens, so it's possible that a dozen generations could share the same home range in an extremely favorable situation, but in this day and age several generations would be more plausible.

Even though fairly large matriarchal groups may share a "home range," the actual social units within the clan remain small if one defines a social unit as a group in more or less constant contact and association. In this case a doe with her fawns of the year and her yearlings of the previous year would constitute a true social unit. When these nuclear families gather with others in open meadows and fields to feed, they may appear to be a larger social herd, but when such aggregations return to bedding sites, they usually break down into family units again.

Although whitetails are not highly gregarious herding beasts, they are nonethe-less social animals that interact regularly with others of their kind and benefit from those interactions. When clan members meet they often touch noses and groom one another about the head and neck. Though there are no regimented training sessions, youngsters learn social behavior, migration routes, localized and seasonal food sources, escape routes and the dominance order merely by traveling with and observing older deer. The hierarchy minimizes stress and fighting over resources. Older and larger deer usually dominate younger, smaller deer. While there is constant low-key jockeying for status, dominance usually changes in an orderly fashion when older females die. Fighting is limited to quick bursts of kicking or flailing, usually when the deer are at concentrated food sources. Normally dominance displays and reciprocal submission displays ward off combat.

STRETCHING BOUNDARIES

Many people think of whitetails as strict homebodies, living within the same square mile or two all their lives. Well, sort of. Where habitat is excellent year-round, such as in parts of the South, a doe might spend her 15 years inside as few as 200 acres. No one knows the absolute minimum because no one has followed a deer every day of its life. But researchers have tagged, radio-collared and studied enough whitetails to know that once they settle in, nothing short of death or complete loss of their habitat (fire, shopping mall, new reservoir, etc.) can push them out. Even under the heaviest hunting pressure they stay home, sneaking and hiding in cover they know best.

A whitetail's home range, however, isn't as neat and clear-cut as a human's backyard or farm.

First, its edges are soft: There's no line in the sand over which the resident deer will not step. It's more of a zone of decreasing visitation, a fuzzy fringe border where the animal spends minimal time and where neighbors often visit. This is also where those displaced yearlings and bucks loiter. The farther this blurry edge is from the heart of the deer's territory, the less it is used.

A buck surveys a chunk of his territory, looking for does. A homebody for much of the year, a buck expands his range significantly during the rut, traveling many miles in search of a ready-and-willing doe.

ADAPTABLE BEHAVIOR

What may be normal whitetail behavior in one part of the country could be unusual in another. Habitat, herd density, intensity of predation and other factors influence local herds and individuals. As a general rule deer in more open country associate in larger groups while those in thick cover tend to be loners or immediate-family units. As many as a hundred related does and fawns might gather loosely to forage in a green field in western Kansas, while more than 10 together would be considered amazing in a Northern forest.

Schedules also vary by region. Tennessee does might jump the gun with mid-May fawning, Northern does might fawn in late May, Florida does might wait until late summer. But in every case fawning is timed to take advantage of some dependable, seasonal abundance that maximizes fawn growth and survival. That's just another example of the whitetail's adaptability.

Second, a whitetail's living quarters are more gerrymandered than geometric. Like a voting district that has been stretched and narrowed to take in a politician's supporting townships and neighborhoods, a deer's home range twists and bends, narrows and widens to take in the best forage, escape cover, fawning grounds, winter cover and travel routes.

Third, not all territories are 2 square miles or less. In the dry West a whitetail might need 6 or even 10 square miles of habitat in order to fill its needs. And bucks almost always roam larger territories than does, usually overlapping the ranges of several matriarchal groups. This gives them more options for seeding their genes.

Fourth, home ranges are seasonal. One section might be used during summer to the exclusion of all others, another only for feeding on acorns during early fall, yet another strictly for wintering. Bucks are notorious for holing up in small core areas for much of the year, then cruising back and forth as many as 20 miles a night during the rut to check the nether reaches of their territories. Out on the Plains, where suitable habitat is often restricted to wooded river bottoms, bucks have been known to move 10 straight-line miles in a night.

Fifth, home ranges are not exclusive territories. Whitetails do not mark boundaries and defend them against all others of their species. Therefore several family units may crisscross the same woods, forage in the same fields, even join into herds from time to time. Even members of different matriarchal clans may feed near one another or intermingle in a communal field. But when it comes time to bed, groups break up into those cozy family units. This is why you often see three or five deer leave the west side of a meadow, cross east and disappear into the brush while five others on the east side of the field go west to bed. The first group may have been on the western edge of their home range, the second on its eastern edge. The separation into family units also explains why we sometimes see long lines of does and fawns leaving fields, but rarely encounter that many together in the woods.

While not strictly territorial, whitetails do recognize strangers and seem to keep them at leg's length. An immigrant doe, for instance, is not welcomed into the local matriarchal group, though she may trail along and feed nearby. She will be tolerated to varying degrees depending on the attitude of the resident alpha female. Yes, even deer exhibit unique "personalities." Some are bold, some cautious. Some are nervous, some calm. And some are just plain ornery. They'll kick and flail at strangers and drive them away from feeding and bedding areas. However, such

If you're a buck, a summer day is for lolling around in some thicket, growing your antlers and waiting for evening when you can venture out to feed again.

interactions are rare because female whitetails rarely leave their own home ranges. Whitetails do not need to defend their territories.

MEANWHILE, BACK AT THE BOYS' RANCH

In midsummer the rarest creature in the woods seems to be the whitetail buck. We know they are there, but we hardly ever see them. That's because the cover is so dense, food so abundant and caloric demands so low. Old bucks in particular are lazy slugs. They've completed their basic body growth, so they don't need to feed as often as lactating does or even young bucks. Warm temperatures and minimal activity equal minimal metabolic demands. There's plenty of time to forage once the sun has set and temperatures have cooled; why walk around in the heat of the day? So they plunk themselves in a shady thicket within their core area, ruminate and vegetate until dark. Then they rise, stretch and saunter to the dinner table, which is often just a bite away. If water is also close, a buck might not stir from a 10-acre patch for days. One hopes they enjoy this vacation because their shift is about to clock in.

Unsuspected by most humans, summering bucks have already begun the rut. Since the previous December they've been competing for breeding rights simply by eating and staying alive. In spring the gastronomic battle heats up, each buck chowing down as much high-quality forage as he can to feed his rapidly growing antlers. This might not sound like a major mating battle, but it is. The fattest, healthiest, best-fed buck grows the biggest antlers and backs them up with the

Above: Velvet peeling.
Below: Summer bachelor band.

heaviest body. This mass intimidates other bucks and knocks them down when push comes to shove. It also carries a male through the frenetic November rut, when he's often too busy spreading his genetic material to eat right. Bigger antlers, bigger body, more stamina. Quite literally he who eats best wins. A mature Dakota buck can enter the rut at a ground-shaking 300 pounds. Some Northern bucks have been weighed at 400 pounds. Among whitetails, summer dining is serious work.

EARLY WAKE-UP CALL

The summer solstice—the longest day/shortest night of the year—is June 21. Immediately thereafter days begin to shorten, and that signals the pituitary gland to gradually wake up the gonads so they can start manufacturing testosterone. By mid- to late July most antlers have already finished growing. By late August they've mineralized and hardened. In early September—still summer—most Northern bucks thrash a few bushes and strip away their velvet. The biggest, healthiest and most testosterone laden males strip first. It's still summer, but already trouble's on the way.

FASHION SHOW?

Long before the real fall rutting action begins, bucks may put on a little fashion show of sorts. Where dense habitat is dotted with sizable openings, especially green feed fields, late summer bucks often creep out of hiding at dusk to stand and feed within view of the doe groups, almost as if giving a preview of upcoming events. *Ladies. How do you do. Ma'am. Miss. Nice evening.* Polite. Subtle. But all the while hoping the new antlers are making the right impression. *Come November, remember me. At your service.* At the same time old bucks who may not have seen one another since the last rut catch glimpses across the field, perhaps even get reacquainted. Everyone meets the new kids on the block and sizes up the competition. Youngsters even indulge in a bit of friendly wrestling. In one way it's like an old-fashioned small town barn dance or ice cream social.

TINE TO SUMO

One wouldn't call a September buck ornery, but he is getting feisty. Temperatures are moderating, he's fed himself up to his prime fighting weight, he's got those new antlers all shined up and, like a boy with a Christmas rifle, he's just itching to try them out. Thus begins the sparring season.

Sparring is usually initiated by young bucks. Nobody's so drunk on testosterone that they want to fight, but all are juiced-up enough to wrestle. So a young, spindly racked 6- or 8-pointer will approach a senior buck with lowered antlers. The old guys recognize this signal and they drop their tines like an old knight acknowledging a challenge to joust.

These young bucks will display their wares to each other—and maybe do a little sparring—to get acquainted and see who's boss.

A recurrent myth among whitetail hunters is that a buck's antlers are stained dark by dried blood after velvet is stripped. Not true: A freshly cleaned antler is quite white. Only after a buck has thrashed brush and made a number of rubs does his rack turn dark, and then mostly near its base. Obviously this is because the base does most of the bark shredding and rubbing, picking up sap, tannin and dirt. Distant tines are often bone white, especially on young bucks who don't do as much thrashing and rubbing as mature males. Late-season bucks show white antlers because rutting behavior has ended and the beams have gradually worn clean.

The contest begins with some tickling of the tines, then some easy neck-twisting, perhaps just a bit of nudging and pushing. Within seconds or minutes it's over. It never gets deadly serious. There's really nothing to fight about. Sparring is just the warm-up for the real matches to come, but it's critically important because it helps young bucks sort things out. By eyeing and then wrestling with a bigger buck's antlers, small bucks learn size/strength relationships. Because their antlers change so dramatically during their first three years, they need to compare. Mature bucks after age 3 or 4 have had enough experience that they can usually assess others' antlers at a glance, so they spar less often.

Most sparring occurs between bucks one age class apart. Even little spikes get in on the act. They gain needed wrestling experience while learning their place within the hierarchy. Sparring may continue for several weeks, the contests heating as time passes. Youngsters even continue through the rut where there are enough old-age bucks in the herd to service all the does. Hey, they've nothing else to do but dream. A bit of practice fighting readies them for the future and probably works off a little immediate tension.

DRESSING UP

Because bucks have minimum energy requirements in midsummer but major demands later, they take advantage of the lull to change into their winter coats.

This buck is fashionably warm in the gray winter coat he started growing during late summer.

The thick, gray winter pelage grows in within four weeks. By mid-September most of the older males are dressed for a blizzard while their mothers, sisters and daughters are still in their thin summer red suits. The females are too busy raising fawns to fool with a new wardrobe. They'll have plenty of time in the fall while the boys are carousing and fighting. Females take the same approach to building their winter fat supply. Bucks hit their peak in late September; does usually peak in November.

RUBBED OUT

Although many hunters associate tree rubs with the rut, bucks start them soon after shedding velvet in the summer. As you might have guessed, testosterone is the driving force behind rubbing. Usually the biggest, strongest buck gets the earliest and biggest dose of the mighty male hormone, so he initiates the rubs. These are not exercise bouts or frustration fights with foliage. Rubs are deliberate visual and olfactory markers, clear signs of a buck's presence and social dominance. A mature buck, "high" on testosterone and full of himself, feels compelled to brag to the world. He rubs trees to do it.

The process is rather simple. The buck selects a tree trunk anywhere from an inch to 12 inches thick, and begins rubbing its bark away with his rough antler bases and brow tines. The pearling acts like a rasp, which may be precisely why antler bases are so rough. With the bark stripped away, the cambium layer, often oozing and sticky, gets a liberal rubbing with the buck's forehead glands. The older and more dominant the buck, the more active his forehead scent glands.

Studies have shown that immature bucks—even in regions with few or no older bucks—don't begin rub-marking until well into October when their testosterone levels have risen and they've had a chance to dominate other young bucks. Even then, young deer don't make nearly as many rubs as do mature males, and they usually select smaller trees. An abundance of large rubs in September, then, clearly signals the presence of a big, prime buck. Few September rubs and small October rubs indicate a poorly managed herd with too few older (at least 3½-year-old) bucks.

A rub works much like a woodsman's blaze for marking a trail. The bright inner bark shines like a beacon in a forest of dark trunks. Deer

Above: Buck rubbing a tree. Rubs are a deliberate visual and olfactory sign marker.
Below: Big rubs are a clear sign that a dominant buck is in the area.

spot this readily. Researchers have stuck man-made "rubs" in whitetail habitat and watched as bucks and does spotted them, approached, sniffed, and sometimes rubbed them. We assume that when deer sniff the bark of a rubbed tree they recognize the odor of a confident, mature buck. The effect on younger males may be to dampen their enthusiasm—sort of like walking past your high school heartthrob's house on Friday night and seeing the Prom King's convertible in her driveway. Rubs don't strictly define territories or chase competitors out, but they could take the wind out of their sails, perhaps even hold their testosterone levels down.

A healthy, mature buck at his rub signpost.

Does, on the other hand, might fire up when they see and smell the signposts. Rubs might help prime all does in a buck's territory. Not surprisingly, bucks rub liberally, sometimes attacking a dozen trees within a single view. They rub along their travel lanes, at places where does congregate, and throughout their stomping grounds.

Although bucks rarely freshen their old rubs, other bucks will indulge, perhaps in an effort to cover up the other's scent and steal his advertisement. Master bucks prefer to mark a fresh tree, often near previous rubs. This creates a cluster of rubs and indicates a favorite travel route, bedding site or staging area near a feed field.

You can just imagine a buck twiddling his thumbs inside the woods bordering a feed field, waiting for darkness before venturing into the open to feed. *Come on sun, set already. Let's go. Let's go.* With time to kill, he rubs a tree. The next night he does the same. After a week or two there may be two dozen rubs along a 100-yard strip. In the morning, back near his core bedding area, the restless buck, not quite ready to hit the hay, makes a few more rubs. So rubs indicate not only that a prime buck is in the area, but also where he spends much of his time—important information if you are a doe anticipating romance or a smaller buck wanting to avoid trouble.

Scraping starts as early as late summer, heralding the frantic activity to come.

From time to time, area bucks "adopt" an official rubbing post, often an old fence post or utility pole, and literally rub it to tinder. Year after year they rasp away at it, gradually carving it to an hourglass shape until a farmer or lineman replaces it or it falls over.

WHAT'S THAT SCRAPING SOUND?

Yes, believe it or not, buck scrapes are another late-summer phenomenon. These are not the big, elaborate breeding scrapes you'll find in November, but smaller spots where a breeder buck has pawed debris down to bare earth. He may or may not urinate down his tarsal glands into the scrape or scent-mark an overhanging limb. Summer scrapes are rare among populations of young bucks, suggesting this behavior is another product of maturity. A buck who has reached his fourth autumn knows the routine, reaches breeding condition early and probably likes to make his mark, get a jump on the competition, deflate the young studs.

Even though breeding is still four to six weeks away, the first rubs and scrapes of the year forecast the end of summer. Good-bye easy living; hello frenetic, exciting, exhausting autumn.

AUTUMN SPLENDOR

From the hunter's perspective autumn is not only the most colorful season but also the most exciting, invigorating and important. Whitetail bucks agree. Does may make their major contribution to the species in spring, but bucks play their big roles during the glorious fall.

After September, ebbing daylight and dropping temperatures inspire creatures great and small to prepare for winter. After the summer doldrums, the first good cold snap brings a flurry of activity. Wildlife populations are at an annual peak. The very air seems alive with excitement. Creatures are caching food, migrating, burrowing and mating.

Whitetails must pile on fat for the lean times to come and, most importantly, sow the seeds for another generation. They feel the impending cold and become the most active they'll be all year, feeding, traveling, posturing, fighting, rubbing, scraping, chasing and rutting up a frenzy. For deer and hunter alike, it's a great season to be alive outdoors.

DELAYED DOES

Whitetail does are less excited by the coming of fall. They don't endure the hormonal changes that ravage bucks at this time. For them, most of autumn is just the long, slow demise of summer and some extra time to fatten up and recover from the tribulations of fawn-rearing. From the autumnal equinox into early November they mostly eat, rest and eat some more. Their biggest chore is growing the winter coat, which comes in so naturally and painlessly one doubts they even realize it's happening. One day they're red and summer sleek, a few weeks later they're gray and thoroughly insulated. Ho hum. Even their fawns are calming down, playing less as they change into their first gray adult coats. With apples, acorns and ripe field grains free for the picking, early autumn is the easiest time of year for a female deer.

FATTENING FAWNS

During this season all deer, even fawns, undergo a physiological shift toward fat production. Since birth they've been growing, but a fat supply is so critical to winter survival that their bodies will interrupt skeletal growth to concentrate on laying fat over the back and hips, around the kidneys and at other places within the gut cavity. Even poorly nourished

LIMB SIGNIFICANCE

The licking branches overhanging scrapes are extremely valuable: without them bucks almost never scrape. Remove one from an active scrape and the scrape will be abandoned. Move one to another location and the first buck that finds it will scrape under it. Biologists have tacked suitably sized scrape limbs to trees where natural limbs were out of reach and bucks quickly turned them into scrapes.

Opposite page: A buck working a licking branch. Below: Autumn is a time of plenty for does, who work hard to fatten up for winter.

Above: During fall,
fawns eat heartily to put
on fat, but, alas, they
are still among the first
to die if winter gets bad.
Opposite page: Rutting
buck with swollen neck.
He's in his prime!

runts make this adjustment, though their chances for survival are small. If they couldn't find enough food to grow properly during early summer, they probably won't find enough to build up a sufficient fat supply, either. This is the cruel price deer pay for living in densities too high for the land to support.

PREPARING FOR CONQUEST

Bucks are busy in October. Having awakened from their summer lethargy, they quickly whip themselves into shape. Testosterone is spiking toward its annual peak and the friendly boys' club is breaking up. The oldest bucks are the first to go solo; youngsters drift away when their hormone levels creep high enough.

Now that antlers are hard, tolerance takes a vacation: No longer can one male live completely at ease with another. Tension builds. Under the influence of testosterone, neck muscles enlarge to impressive proportions. Bucks start fidgeting, pacing, roaming far and wide, thrashing shrubs and saplings, shadowboxing into top shape. Sparring matches grow heated. The gentle boys of summer have become "whitetails with attitude."

STUCK IN A RUT—ALMOST

This period between antler hardening and the beginning of breeding is known as the pre-rut. Bucks seek to accomplish three things during this time: 1. Intimidate other bucks and rise to the top of the pecking order; 2. Advertise themselves to as many does as possible; 3. Find and claim the first ready female.

This rutting buck is hot on the trail of a doe. No time to slow down now! A buck on a scent trail is like a bloodhound on the hunt, his nose glued to the trail, following wherever it might lead. He'll often grunt all the way.

Nature has set up the ways in which males pursue these goals, yet the process changes in different parts of the country. This is because "typical" behavior hinges on normal herd age structure and sex ratios. In states where bucks are consistently overharvested they rarely grow old enough to perfect and exhibit their masculine behaviors. Expecting a 1½-year-old whitetail to rub and scrape and properly court females is like expecting a 13-year-old boy to grow a mustache, hold down a man's job and take a grown woman to the opera. In the absence of mature bucks, youngsters do more chasing and harassing than advertising and courting. This is why you see spikes and spindly six-points nosing and chasing does in open fields at noon in October. The older guys know enough to wait until November when their efforts will bear fruit.

OH WHERE HAVE YOU BEEN BUCKY BOY, BUCKY BOY?

Where there are biologically normal ratios of young and old, bucks and does, the prime (4- to 8-year-old) stags begin making scrapes at traditional doe concentration spots (October in the North, as late as November or even December in parts of the South). A mature buck will know these productive "trolling" spots from past experience—a copse of trees near a feed field, a thicket of pines on a hardwood ridge, a lush bottom near oak woods, the confluence of several major trails. Some of these hotspots might be miles from his core area, but he makes the long trip to increase his odds for breeding success.

This might be the only time of the year he visits these distant fringes of his territory. It's dangerous work. Our wandering hero is exploring unfamiliar, though

not unknown, places where predators lurk and bright lights leap out of the blackness. More whitetails are road-killed during fall than any other season, and a disproportionate number are bucks on the prowl.

As he travels, the veteran will pause to rub a sapling here and there as a calling card to females and a warning to males. If he bumps into other bucks, all sorts of things can happen. If it is a familiar face (they can recognize one another by their antlers as well as odors) both animals might glance and go, as if late for a business luncheon. Other times they might stay together and feed side by side for an hour. They might spar for a few minutes. Sometimes three or four get together like guys at a sports bar after work. The sight of two going at it often inspires the other two to start up. Occasionally tempers rise and a good-natured wrestling match turns ugly, both contestants thinking they have the opportunity to move up the social ladder. Infrequently a third buck, worked into a frenzy by the sight of the battle, will suddenly blind-side one of the fighters, severely wounding or killing him. The sounds of clicking antlers and stomping hooves often lure distant bucks to the arena. It seems no one, not even deer, can resist a good fight.

While conducting their October rounds, strangers sometimes meet at the far edges of their respective territories. They may cautiously work closer, sniff, posture and attempt to establish dominance. The more aggressive male—usually the one with

Above: Experienced bucks know where does congregate. Below: This rutting buck has taken a tine in the eye.

Bucks spar as a test to determine where each fits in the social hierarchy. Rather than a knock-down, drag-out fight, these tests of strength are ritualized and seldom involve injury.

the biggest body, biggest rack and most testosterone—will display typical dominance body language: ears laid back, head low with antlers projected forward, body hairs erect, walking stiff-legged. If the other buck doesn't object, he'll turn away and keep his fur flat. *Okay. You win.* End of conflict. But not always, as we'll discuss later.

THE 10 PERCENT RISK

Biologists have determined that approximately 10 percent of each year's buck population dies from fighting injuries such as tine punctures, locked antlers and infections. This suggests that no bucks would live past 9 years, yet some do. This is because most don't fight seriously for their first season or two and some, after the age of 8 or so, opt out of the rut altogether. Then there are what we might call "chicken" bucks (and they might call "smart" bucks) that rarely fight at all. They have an excellent chance of dying of old age—if they aren't eaten by predators, four-legged or two.

JUST SCRAPING BY

The older the buck and the later the date, the less he'll mess with other males. It's more important that he keep circulating, advertising, looking for willing partners of the opposite sex. By early November he's like the mailman, making the rounds, dropping off messages, checking for replies. His mailbox is his scrape, that 2- to 3-foot diameter oval he paws on the ground and urinates into. Exactly why bucks scrape is their secret, but after decades of scrutiny, researchers suspect it's to discourage other bucks, encourage estrus in does, and perhaps provide a way for ripe females to get in touch.

Scientists do know that scraping is instinctive behavior, but it must be practiced and perfected. If you were a deer, here's how you would go about it.

A branch that's four to six feet off the ground must be present before a buck will create a scrape. Move the overhead branch and the scrape will be abandoned. Set up an overhead branch in another spot and the bucks may move to that location.

Locate a limb four to six feet off the ground along a well-used doe travel corridor or loafing spot—feeding field edges, trail junctions, bedding sites and narrow strips of trees between larger wood lots are good bets. Chew off the tip of the limb or break it to expose a rough end. You might twist it in your antler tines to help with this. Now mouth it, lick it, poke it into your nose gland, rub it into your preorbital gland, maybe give it a pass or two over your forehead. Now use your front hooves to paw down to bare dirt directly underneath this limb. Rake away all the leaves and grass. Now step into the scrape with all four feet, rub your tarsal hairs together and urinate down your legs. Now, if there is a lot of doe scent in the area, move over to the next limb and scrape again. It's permissible to cluster a dozen scrapes into a pretty small area. In fact, there's no official limit; maybe you can set a new record.

The more charged with testosterone a buck is and the higher he sits on the dominance scale, the earlier and more frequently he will scrape. Just like rub behavior. And, like rubs, scrapes are rare in overhunted herds. Yearling bucks might make

A mature northern forest buck clearing away leaves while making a scrape.

one scrape for every 10 a prime stag paws out, and they probably won't be nearly as big. Scraping frequency varies widely among mature stags, probably according to testosterone levels and competition from other males. It only makes sense that an abundance of breeder bucks would inspire each to try harder.

Scrape use is erratic. A buck might freshen a scrape each night for a week, then abandon it for eight days, then hit it again. Or he might never touch it again. Generally when does start coming into heat a prime buck is too busy wooing to check his mail. Some studies have shown that mature bucks "tune up" about half their scrapes at least once. Some are used annually for years and by succeeding males, reflecting the standard philosophy of real estate—location, location, location.

OPEN TO ALL COMERS

One buck's scrape may have a variety of effects on other bucks. The "alpha buck" theory holds that no lesser buck touches a master buck's scrape. Instead they approach cautiously, tails between their legs, sniffing for clues, hoping to find a doe while the big guy is away. Sometimes they carve a wide berth downwind around the scrape site, afraid to even come within view until they know the coast is clear. If it is, they usually step up and contribute their own scent to both the licking branch and the dirt circle. In this regard scrapes are communal property, sort of like fire hydrants serve dogs. All comers give it a squirt of their identifying scent.

Bucks that swagger up to scrapes are presumed to be the master or his equal. Surprisingly, puny-racked yearlings often waltz right in and dance all over a scrape, sometimes even rolling in it. Probably they're just too stupid to know they're playing with dynamite. In many locales even the king stag checks his scrapes by nose from well downwind, never bothering to approach unless he catches an intoxicating aroma. This may reflect local hunting pressure as much as natural behavior.

It has been discovered that, at least in some parts of the country, mature bucks visit their scrapes at night 80 percent of the time. Of the 20 percent daylight visits, the majority occur at midmorning and midafternoon rather than dawn or dusk.

Scientists are still exploring how does use scrapes. Some biologists insist does visit scrapes when ready to breed, urinate in them, hang around, and leave an obvious scent trail when they finally leave. Then the buck makes his rounds, hits the lucky number, sticks his nose to the ground and trots off. Boy meets girl and extinction is postponed. Other researchers and treestand hunters who watch scrapes for thousands of hours contend, however, that such scenarios are fairly uncommon. Or perhaps they do it at night. The fact that bucks rarely check their scrapes once estrus has kicked in suggests they don't depend on them for getting lucky.

ANCIENT MATCHMAKER'S TRICK

Scraping as a way to play matchmaker may be an evolutionary adaptation to accommodate sparse populations. These days many whitetail populations are so dense that bucks can't see their scrapes without first shooing a hundred does out of the way. But a million years ago, when competition from more predators plus dozens more large herbivores probably held whitetail populations at low densities, scraping may have been critical for bringing young lovers together.

A mature, dominant buck scent-checks his scrape. He can tell if does or other bucks have been in the area.

PIGGING OUT

The amount of time does and fawns spend eating in late fall seems excessive. They'll routinely begin feeding at dawn and stay at it until midmorning. By late afternoon they're back at it, continuing until dark. Since they feel secure enough in the dark to bed in the open, they lay right where they've fed to ruminate until it's time to get up and forage again, usually twice a night. All of this pigging out is necessary, of course. The more energy they can store as fat, the better their chances for pulling through winter.

Left: This doe has a mouthful and will have many more before winter hits.

Above: The limb above a scrape provides a buck with a place to advertise that he is patrolling the area. He rubs his forehead and preorbital glands on it, depositing his scent. Often the buck gently mouths the limb, other times he vigorously thrashes the branch with his antlers.

MUCH ADO ABOUT NOTHING—MAYBE

For years the preorbital gland has been hyped as a primary scent-marker of licking branches, but some scientists question this. They point out that bucks much more frequently and consistently mouth and rub their noses on licking branches than they rub their preorbitals. And preorbitals don't ooze wax or oil, certainly no more during rut than at any other time of year. No definitive studies have absolutely proved or disproved these ideas. That's the beauty and mystery of whitetails. Even though they are probably the most intensively studied big game animals on Earth, they still keep their secrets.

THIS AIN'T NO BACHELOR PAD

Contrary to one theory, a cluster of scrapes does not identify a buck's "breeding territory." No stag in his right mind is going to stand around his collection of scrapes when he can cruise the woods and hunt for action. His mission is to breed. If he happens to make a date at one of his many scrapes, great. But he'll just as happily indulge a pretty young thing he happens to meet at the salad bar two miles away. Bucks wouldn't be cruising day and night to the far corners of their ranges if they were using discreet breeding territories. Instead they'd stay home, defend their bachelor pads from all comers, and be ready with candles and wine when the ladies showed up.

While some macho bucks begin scraping as early as September, most don't get serious until mid-October. Scraping peaks during the two weeks before the area's first doe comes into heat. Across the bulk of whitetail range north of Tennessee, this falls sometime between October 20 and November 20. Once the females start accepting gentlemen callers, scrapes are nearly abandoned. Teenagers and boys might still check them, but the old herd sires are too busy to bother. By the time they're done servicing one doe, they barely have time to clear the fog from their heads before they catch scent of another.

In some places scraping resumes about two weeks after breeding begins. By this time most does have bred, but energetic bucks will freshen and check their old scrapes in hopes of attracting a late bloomer. In the most productive habitats, where food is abundant and superior, female fawns often reach their first estrus by mid-December. Any older does that didn't conceive also recycle for another try after about 28 days.

RUB-A-DUB-DUB

Along with scraping, bucks keep making rubs, too, for the usual reasons. They're leaving their mark, bragging about their vigor, warning the competition to slow down and back off. Many observers insist that bucks also vent excess energy and frustration when they rub, but we have no proof of this. As long as testosterone levels remain high, bucks keep rubbing. It's just a part of their nature.

Given the choice, does prefer mature and experienced bucks. This male courts delicately, slowly licking around the doe's rump. At this point she is probably willing to stand for mounting.

FIGHT OR FLIGHT

By the time does are finally ready to mate, resident bucks have pretty much sorted things out. They've seen and smelled one another again and again. They've sparred and fought. They know who to challenge and who to defer to. But once the intoxicating fragrance of a ready doe wafts on the evening breeze, all hell can break lose. If a bordering buck catches the signal and follows its source into another buck's territory, the two strangers have a good chance of meeting. If they're evenly matched, a serious fight can break out—quickly.

This is not the polite sparring of October, nor is it a brief altercation between known entities. This is destiny, or at least each buck's chance for it. With nothing to go on but antler and body size, each beast sizes up his opponent and either bows out or escalates the encounter. First the display: They stare at each other. Erect hairs to maximize size. Lower antlers, lay ears back and down along the neck. They grunt. Hiss. Sidle toward each other, stiff-legged. *I'm not bluffing buddy. Better git while the gittin' is good.*

The other may break off the impending battle simply by turning away. But he doesn't. They glare at each other. *Better git yourself. I could take you with one antler tied behind my back. This doe is mine. Not in my backyard!*

And then one charges. They crash together viciously, full speed, necks twisting, feet digging and legs driving. Each tries to push the other down, to slip past and gore his adversary, kill him. The display of power and expenditure of energy is awesome and extravagant. The battle may rage for seconds, minutes, or even an hour. Tines might snap like two-by-fours. The bucks grunt, bawl, slobber, hiss and puff. When one feels his antagonist weaken he presses the attack, trying to throw this

Altercations can break out between known opponents during the rut, but the episodes are usually brief. All-out, to-the-death fights usually occur between two evenly matched strangers vying for a hot doe.

DEFEAT OF GOLIATH

More than once hunters have watched a smaller buck whip a larger one. How can this happen?

There are at least two possible reasons. One is that some deer are simply meaner and tougher than others. Just like some humans. They might not be the biggest or strongest, but they make up in aggression what they lack in power. So, a hard-charging, back-'em down little buck can sometimes defeat a larger, stronger buck by sheer force of will.

And sometimes the smaller deer is in better shape. A master buck with huge antlers might be flat worn out toward the end of the rut when a smaller buck in better condition challenges him. It's a simple case of kicking a good stag when he's down. To avoid this, some older deer simply stop rutting and go into seasonal retirement when they run out of steam. Such worn-out bucks are usually the first to shed their antlers, too, because their testosterone levels fall quickly.

enemy to the ground, crush him. Bucks have been seen to lift others clear off the ground, even throw them over their own backs, snapping off their antlers at the base, or at the skull plate.

If a loser is lucky he can disengage, whirl and run before being punctured. The victor will usually chase and attempt to drive home the victory, but usually not more than a few yards. Sometimes two warriors lock antlers in a fatal embrace. Unable to free themselves, they slowly starve to death or get eaten alive by coyotes. More than one buck has been found dragging around the picked-clean skeleton or head of another.

While the battle rages, the fetching little doe who started it all is probably off flirting with a different buck altogether.

EENY MEENY MINEY MOE

There is considerable speculation and some evidence that does select their mates rather than vice versa. This doesn't fit the image of the commanding, virile stud buck, but until a doe agrees to stand for a mating, it isn't going to happen. So how and when do they decide to stand? How do they pick the lucky guy?

Does probably use a "fitness test" of sorts to choose a mate. Typically does become extraordinarily active as they near estrus. They pace their home ranges incessantly, increasing their walking time almost 30 times more than normal. They hang out around scrape sites and urinate frequently in little spurts so as to leave as many scent messages as possible. When bucks catch these olfactory come-hither hints, they pick up the trail. But the pair does not sail off on a quiet honeymoon yet. Instead the female continues wandering, playing coy with her suitor, dashing

away when he approaches too closely. Immature bucks don't understand the program. Driven by scents, hormones and strange urges, they prance too close, spook the doe and chase her.

Again and again they pursue until the poor female is forced to urinate to make her escape. A buck will always stop to sniff the discharge, then curl his upper lip in the famous Flehmen display. This somehow helps him detect her readiness. While he's so engrossed, she runs away.

Where there are plenty of bucks, a train often forms, as many as a half-dozen studs following one little doe. This works to her advantage. The more attention she attracts, the greater her pool of potential partners. The chase may last for hours. Bucks that can't keep up are justifiably winnowed out: No need to saddle the next generation with slow genes. When the doe stops, the boys jockey for position, the largest chasing off the smaller contestants. More winnowing ensues. She wants a confident, powerful mate. She may also pay special attention to the antlers because big antlers signify several useful genetic traits, all of which contribute to longevity.

But antlers alone don't win the courting contest. Nor does brute strength. If size and strength alone determined fatherhood, whitetails would gradually grow larger, bulkier and stronger. That's great for mature males fighting over females, but it doesn't help fawns and does trying to run

Once a buck locates a doe in estrus he will stay with her until she's ready to breed, chasing off all other deer including her young of the year.

GO AWAY, KIDS

When does come into heat they probably do not chase their fawns away, but by the time the bucks get through chasing and harassing her, the family is split just the same. The youngsters, alarmed at this heretofore unheard of behavior, not to mention the sheer size and frightening rushes of the bucks, simply spook and head for cover. Separation lasts but a few days at most. Mom stays within her home range, and once she's bred she and the youngsters find each other again, the family returns to its normal routine.

away from predators. Somehow these deer must strike a balance between agility, speed and strength. By leading a string of bucks on a wild chase, the doe selects for all those qualities.

Mature bucks know the mating game and show some reserve, standing patiently at a distance, moving in slowly, cautiously, one step at a time, letting the gal get used to them. This is called tending. Tending bucks often grunt repeatedly, sounding like happy pigs. The purpose of these grunts is anybody's guess. Perhaps they reassure and relax the female. Maybe they warn other bucks to stay clear, though this seems unlikely as they would surely attract bucks—maybe much larger ones. Perhaps the buck is so full of anticipation he simply can't contain himself.

If possible, a tending buck herds his doe to an empty corner of her home range, a quiet honeymoon suite where they won't likely be disturbed by jealous rivals. He grunts as he follows, holding his head low and his nose forward so his threatening tines are held back. From time to time he snorts and rushes her, causing her to urinate. He sniffs the liquid for readiness, lip curling in apparent ecstasy. When he judges the time is right, he presses his suit. She stands, lets him rub his neck on her back, her rump. He flicks his tongue, licks and grooms her. She licks him. Probably the two are imitating doe-fawn interactions, which might reassure the smaller doe that this hulking buck with the dangerous antlers won't maul her.

Opposite page: A western buck performs a lip-curl or flehmen, enjoying the whiff of doe-in-heat he's getting. Above: Two bucks vying for a doe's attention display typical aggressive poses: with ears laid back, they walk stiff-legged, broadside to the doe.

Buck and doe copulating in the Montana foothills. He may love her and leave her, or he may stick around for a day at the most, doing his duty once or twice more.

Copulation occurs quickly. The stag is up and down in seconds. He may require several preliminary attempts, but once he gets it right, it's generally all over until next year. Some does will permit a second or third mounting. The estrus period usually lasts only 24 hours. Then the buck is off on another conquest and the doe rejoins her fawns to resume her important autumn duty: eating.

TOO TIRED TO TANGO

Eager as bucks are to spread their genes, they do have their limits. When a herd's age and sex ratios are reasonably balanced there is tough competition for breeding rights. Prime bucks expend considerable energy maintaining scrapes, searching for does, fighting one another and, finally, breeding as many females as they can. For nearly two months they've been going nonstop. By late November many have lost literally all the fat and body mass they'd gained over the summer; they have little

HEY, A MAN'S GOTTA EAT, DOESN'T HE?

You know that old saying about bucks not eating during the rut? Well, it's not quite accurate. They eat. But not much. Certainly not enough to maintain their weight. Perfectly healthy, mature bucks have been recorded losing nearly 30 percent of their pre-rut weight by the end of the breeding period.

Knowing how nature provides for creatures, this seems a bit foolish. Couldn't she have arranged things so bucks could complete their duties at a time of year when food is more available? By the time the rut finishes over most of the North, the snow is already flying—not an easy time to try to regain weight.

Not surprisingly, there is a method to this madness. Since bucks are superfluous to the population once they've planted the seeds for the next generation, they can be sacrificed with minimum impact on the population. In fact, fewer mouths to feed in a wintering yard might enable another doe or two to survive with their twin fawns.

This might not sound like a great plan if you're a buck, but it's served the species well for at least 4 million years, so it can't be all bad.

energy left. The bucks are skinny, scarred, tattered and bleeding. Many have had tines or even entire antlers snapped off. Some have lost ear tips and eyes. Is it any wonder some opt to call it a season? By Thanksgiving the biggest, baddest, randiest monarch in the county might be happy to simply limp into the densest cover he can find and vegetate. Experienced observers believe such bucks literally hole up for days, barely moving. At most they ease out under cover of darkness to feed, then creep back into the shadows to sleep out the day, wholly disinterested in sex. *What's that? Some fresh young fillies have come into estrus? Big deal. Who cares. Let someone else put up with them. I'm beat.* This physiological reality gives other bucks a chance and broadens the gene pool. It may also preserve a few bucks—the bigger, older, smarter, dominant ones—for one more year.

This mature midwestern buck is totally exhausted after the rut. Bucks like this may hole up for days to recover. Then it's time to binge feed, trying to lay on some fat before winter hits.

HANGING ON—WINTER

The mission for northern deer: just survive. Fat reserves are the key. Deer eat, but intake rarely exceeds output. Weight loss of 20 to 25 percent is common.

After the flurry of autumn, northern whitetails enter their low season. The light is low, temperatures are low, food supplies are low, even the deer's spirits are low. Fawns do not play during winter; adults run only when they have to. Their winter mission is to survive—often through deep snows, intense cold and minimum forage for three or four months. The less energy they waste, the greater the chances they'll see another spring.

Minimizing activity is so critical to a whitetail's winter survival that it is built into its physiology. Decreasing daylight signals the thyroid gland to slow down, and that shifts metabolism and behavior into low gear. A deer's body begins a fat-metabolizing modus operandi similar to that of a hibernating bear. The quantity of fat stored during fall often determines survival. Deer continue to feed in winter, but intake rarely exceeds output. Now, whitetails usually consume only 70 percent of their normal daily ration. Even when kept under controlled conditions and given free access to all the highest quality hay and grains

BUCKS ON THE OUTSIDE

Researchers have learned that mature bucks tend to live on the edges of winter yards while does take the middle. Apparently bucks would rather stay near better forage than near better thermal insulation. They can afford to do this given their larger body size and slower metabolism. But they need more food because after the rut they are rarely as fat as does. Even though they tend to live in small bachelor groups, bucks risk increased predation since there are fewer "guards" on duty. They also have fewer trails to run in. To compensate, they bed near small ridge tops near dense escape cover where they can more effectively see and smell approaching danger.

they want, whitetails lose weight until spring green-up. In the wild a 20 to 25 percent weight loss is common, and some deer have survived 30 percent losses.

Obviously, with this kind of stress and deprivation, minimizing energy output becomes critical. Most energy is needed just to generate body heat, so conservation is essential. Winter deer cut their normal activity by half. They walk only as far as they must to eat and bed. They lie for hours without moving. Fortunately there are no flies to swat. Snow piles up on their backs. They sleep more than usual. (Apparently winter lethargy isn't just a human phenomenon.)

Because of increased energy loss and decreased energy gain, where a deer decides to spend his winter days becomes critical—sometimes more critical than what he eats.

LET IT SNOW?

Snow is a mixed blessing to deer. It slows them down when predators attack, but it insulates and provides a ready source of water. Sometimes it settles heavily on boughs and bends them within reach. It provides life-giving moisture when water is frozen. And when it melts it irrigates that critical spring vegetation, the first real food a deer might have tasted in three months.

A VARIETY OF WINTER HABITATS

In the forested Northeast, deer migrate toward traditional winter yards in conifer thickets of spruce, balsam fir, hemlock and northern white cedar for the cover and weather protection they provide. Each generation learns of these places by following older deer—usually mothers, grandmothers or sisters. They may travel as many as 40 miles but usually no more than 10 to reach these cozy winter homes. In the northern Rockies whitetails sometimes just drop from a mountaintop to a valley, or

In winter, whitetails reduce normal activities and lie unmoving for hours. Note the snow that has accumulated on this buck's insulating hair.

TOP DOG

Forget Bambi. Forget all that soft, cuddly, romantic nonsense about the gentle beasts. It's dog-eat-dog, or rather bigger-deer-kick-little-deer, in the winter yard when food is scarce.

Humans like to pretend that nature is kind and fair and only mankind is unkind. Reality contradicts this. Humans are among the few species that will sacrifice themselves for the good of the group. Bucks won't fight to defend their brothers; a doe won't give up food so her sister can eat. It's every deer for him or herself. This includes fawns at the browse pile. Any deer will bully away a smaller deer to get food. And yes, a doe will drive off her own fawns. It isn't pretty. It isn't kind. But it is. Survival of the fittest is indeed the name of the game.

Opposite page: This fawn depends on the good judgment of its mother to guide it through winter. Fawns learn the location of winter yards by following their mothers on the migration route. Following pages: Because these Wyoming does' digestive systems are used to the forage, these hay bales are probably doing them some good.

slide from a north-facing slope to a sun-drenched south slope next to irrigated farm fields. On the Plains they march in from broad grain fields dotted with patches of escape cover to forested riverbottoms or dense farmland shelterbelts near haystacks or cornfields.

Yarding usually connotes large concentrations of deer locked into a small area—100 to several hundred acres—by deep snow. As the herd plows through the snow in search of food it creates an interlacing system of trails that subsequently make travel easier and save everyone energy. Plains whitetails often don't confine themselves to such small areas or don't need to tramp out snow paths. They may bed in little patches of brush and trees but usually hike a mile or two to reach waste corn, winter wheat plants, alfalfa or haystacks. The deeper the snow, the more often they raid hay. High quality forage makes up for the extra energy expended to reach it. Because Plains deer from across broad summer ranges are forced into limited winter habitat, they often coalesce into sizable herds.

The abundance of corn and soybeans in northern farm states has created an unusual opportunity for whitetails. These grains provide so much energy that deer can bed nearby in the skimpiest cover and survive the winter. Often they lie right out in the open fields. It's a nice system until a blizzard hits. If grains get buried and there are no woods nearby with adequate browse, local deer are in big trouble. Local populations can be completely wiped out as happened in parts of North and South Dakota during the interminable 1996–97 winter with its record snows.

In the middle states and Midwest farm country, snow often isn't deep enough to force any sort of yarding behavior. In some heavily farmed areas whitetails are forced to migrate to nearby river bottoms for adequate winter cover. Ideally resident deer merely shift to denser cover within their normal home ranges and continue scouring the woods for acorns, the fields for waste grain or cured vegetation and the thickets for woody browse. Intermittent deep snows might hem them in for a few days, but it usually melts to free them before they get too hungry.

Southern deer are limited more by late-winter flooding than anything else. This causes hardship because the richest, most nutritious forage grows in the alluvial bottomlands. Ridge vegetation is usually poor quality. Fortunately winter crops like wheat are usually available to provide quality dining. When flood waters recede, resident deer migrate back to their traditional home ranges.

In the drier parts of Texas, deer face a unique winter challenge: drought. After a hot summer, vegetation is often sparse and dried out. Fortunately, a variety of scrub species remain nutritious, and prickly pear cacti provide both nutrition and

For this Texas buck, drought may be the survival challenge that winter presents.

moisture until rain finally brings fresh forbs. South Texas deer stay much more active than Northern deer. They have to, because the peak of their rut falls between the middle of December and early January.

Extreme Southeastern whitetails also rut in late December. Woody browse is abundant in most areas, and early agricultural crops provide plenty to eat. In many forests and swamplands, however, overpopulation puts severe pressure on forage. Scrawny and stunted deer are often the result.

YARDING

The obvious reasons for yarding are snow and wind protection plus availability of winter browse. Once snow depth reaches a foot, whitetails have a tough time digging down to cured plants, grains or acorns. They must shift to woody limbs, buds and boughs. In the North, white cedar is the most nutritious browse, sufficient in itself to fuel a deer until spring. Balsam, dogwood, aspen, maple and most other shrubs and trees are barely more than fillers. They are tough to digest and may be low in protein, carbohydrates and fat. Some plants contain oils that interfere with microbial digestion. To survive on browse, a deer must enter winter well-fatted, eat a lot, eat a variety, keep movement to a minimum and stay out of the cold wind.

Insulation is another important function of a wintering yard. An overstory of evergreen boughs catches snow, keeping the ground open so deer don't have to struggle through deep snow. Tall, dense evergreens also cover the air mass like a giant blanket. Low boughs block winds. Temperatures inside a cedar swamp might average just one or two degrees higher than outside, but reduction of wind makes a major difference to the inhabitants. A major blizzard with gusts of 30 mph could be blowing across clear-cuts and open fields, but deep within a cedar swamp the air is practically still. The effect is a cozy microclimate. Just by keeping breezes off their backs, whitetails save considerable energy while staying warm. Wrapped in their thick winter coats, curled in a snow hole beneath a balsam bough, whitetails are about as snug as an ungulate can be outside of a heated barn or tropical jungle.

ICE AIN'T NICE

As far as whitetails are concerned, there's nothing good about ice. It locks up drinking water, and when hard hooves try to walk on it, it provides no traction. Deer trying to cross slick ice often splay out their legs and dislocate or break their hips. Sometimes they break through ice and drown or slip off into rivers and get swept away. Of course, sometimes ice provides a route across a river or reservoir to better forage on the far side. Like gravity it's just there. They deal with it.

The worst of winter is yet to come. In thick forest, whitetails use a network of paths to save valuable energy while traveling to feeding and resting areas.

ALL THIS & DINNER TOO

The ideal yard combines shelter with food, all from the same tree—the white cedar. A wilderness bed and breakfast. Sadly, deer numbers have been so bloated for so long in most of the North that they've stripped many cedar swamps of all reachable browse. Look at a northern Wisconsin or Michigan cedar thicket and you'll see an obvious, straight browse line 6 to 7 feet from the ground. This not only deprives deer of food but opens the understory to whistling winds, wiping out just about all the swamp's wintering value.

When yard browse is scarce or gone, deer are forced to wander beyond the yard's edges in search of a meal. The farther they go, the more energy they waste. If they leave the protective overstory or trail system, they face deeper snow and burn even more precious internal fuel. The

BROWSE SIZE

The nutrition in woody browse is found in the cambium layer and the buds. The woody core is impossible to digest. Whitetails prefer toothpick- to match-sized browse. When they begin crunching off pencil-sized stems, we know they're desperately hungry.

A buck paws away snow to get at some browse. The severity of the winter, more than any other factor, determines which deer will survive to pass on their genes to future generations.

longer they search between bites, the more energy they waste. And while they're searching and browsing, the wind and cold pull still more heat from their bodies. It's a vicious cycle that can only be ended by reducing herd size for years to let natural vegetation recover.

ANY PORT IN A STORM

Loggers in northern Idaho feel pretty good about assisting wintering whitetails. When they fell a large Douglas fir, hemlock or pine, long ribbons of hanging lichens come down with the branches. Hungry deer relish these. Sometimes they creep from the forest to start feeding while chainsaws still whine nearby.

Deer in the Northeast are also attracted to logging sites where they feed on the trimmed branches. A cutting operation beside a winter yard can be the salvation of an entire herd during a long winter, though it is no permanent solution. A herd that depends on felled trees for food is hopelessly out of balance with its resources. When all the nearby trees are down, the herd is back to facing starvation. If they move farther and farther afield to reach other logging operations, they lose more energy to the hike and cold than they gain from the forage. The only long-term solution is to keep populations within the carrying capacity of winter habitat.

LONG-TERM RELATIONSHIPS

It is possible for cedar swamps to sustain generations of deer over long periods of time. Some Northeast yards have been in continuous use for a hundred years or more. Whitetails are as faithful to these wintering yards as to their summer ranges. This is, after all, part of their home range. Many deer become so attached to winter yards that they stay and starve rather than explore nearby areas for alternative food or even to escape predators. In this regard they walk a tightrope: Is it better to stay on starvation rations and minimize energy expenditure or leave and find more food? Are you safer from predators on your maze of trails, or could you hide from them far from the obvious yard?

ARTIFICIAL FEEDING DEBATE

For decades sportsmen's groups and compassionate deer lovers have argued with biologists about winter feeding. It seems obvious to many that you save starving deer by feeding them. Sometimes biologists are such insensitive dunderheads.

Well, it might not feel right to stand by and let deer starve, but feeding them isn't really the right answer, either. By the time most folks recognize the problem, it's usually too late. The deer are too far gone to save. Other times people provide food that the local whitetails' gut flora can't digest. On occasion, feeding has lured deer to the edges of highways or open fields where they became road kill, were attacked by dogs or simply spent so much energy getting to and from the food that they used up more energy than they gained.

But all of these problems can be fixed with a proper feeding program: one that starts early in winter, is conducted close to traditional dense bedding cover, provides a variety of forage and continues until spring green-up.

Yet the real problem with artificial feeding is that it promotes overpopulation. If deer are starving, chances are it's not because the snow is unusually deep, but because they've been allowed to proliferate until they've mowed down all the winter browse. Feeding them just makes subsequent winters even worse.

Finally, even the best-intentioned, best-maintained and best-conducted feeding can lead to big trouble. In Michigan, artificial feeding (which concentrates deer and leads to frequent contact between them) spread tuberculosis to many animals one winter. That potentially devastating disease could affect not only tens of thousands of deer but also livestock.

So we're back to the point those hard-hearted biologists always make: A natural system that provides adequate cover and adequate food for a reasonable number of deer is best. Work to improve natural food sources and increase natural habitat; that will do more in the long run than any amount of artificial feeding.

THE BIG BAD WOLF

The slowest and weakest are usually the first deer taken by predators, like these Minnesota wolves.

There is no doubt that a communal yard provides significant protection from predators despite its obviousness. Once the Big Bad Wolf discovers a deer yard, he's done hunting for weeks. Now all he has to do is catch. But that might not be as easy as we'd think.

With so many deer in a small area, each animal's odds of avoiding wolves, cougars or feral dogs are high. Lots of eyes, ears and noses are watching. The sudden explosion of a dozen deer, dashing and flashing hither and yon, confuses predators, and while they try to sort things out, the deer often get away. And, of course, the trail system makes it easier for a deer to run. Once snow depth reaches a deer's belly, it is nearly helpless. Natives and pioneers used to chase whitetails down and club them after deep snowfalls. When deep snow begins to crust, predators can run on top while sharp-hoofed deer break through and flounder.

Even without deep snow, though, they don't all get away. In fact, wolves are pretty efficient at taking whitetails—even the biggest bucks still in hard antler. Coyotes and bobcats get a few too. The slowest and weakest deer are usually taken first. The old, arthritic does and bucks function as sacrificial lambs, assuaging the ravenous beasts. These deer were unlikely to contribute anything more to the herd anyway. They'd had their day in the sun. With them out of the way there is more food for younger deer and pregnant does which are the future of the herd.

Prime bucks, however, are also taken in high numbers because they are often

It's sad but true: This fuzzy-faced fawn, whose hair stands on end to offer maximum insulation, may be the first to go, making room for a mature deer that's more likely to survive and breed successfully next fall.

weakened from the rut. Still, this is another reasonable tradeoff. A skinny stag is not likely to pull through on starvation rations, but because he's physically larger than does, he dominates them in the lunch line. When food is concentrated and scarce, he eats first. Starving a doe carrying twin fawns to feed a scrawny old buck is not good livestock management. Besides, he has already contributed his genes to perhaps a dozen or more fawns over the years; if he's sacrificed, a pregnant doe can live.

Fawns are the mothers and fathers of the future, full of potential. Must they die before they've even had a chance to contribute to the herd? Apparently. If a fawn dies, a mature doe lives—and she may be carrying two fawns. She is also fatter so more likely to withstand the coming cold. She is taller and better able to reach the higher browse. She is stronger and faster and more likely to outrun the wolves.

Bucks will sometimes band together again come winter, congregating in traditional wintering haunts and tolerating each other's presence again.

THE DEADLIEST MONTH

Because March brings the first big thaws, humans in the North tend to breathe easier, thinking winter's worst is over. But this is actually the hardest time for whitetails. Their fat reserves are used up, they're at their weakest, and their metabolism shoots up again. They need food and they need lots of it, yet few plants will sprout until April.

If the snow is gone, deer can spread out and find fresh browse far from the overused yards. However, one of those all-too-common March blizzards can roar in and catch them in the open. It's a difficult month for whitetails because they are at peak stress for the year. And that makes it a good time for humans and their dogs to stay out of the woods.

When wolves, cats or coyotes take deer, especially from an overpopulated herd, they are helping to restore habitat deer require to survive over the long haul. When deer starve to death it is only after they've severely compromised their habitat. This sets the stage for another grim winter, year after year. In some parks and protected areas where neither wolves nor human hunters trim the whitetail herd, preferred forage plants have been wiped out, along with some of the small mammals and songbirds that depend on them.

TOO MUCH OF A GOOD THING

Winter overbrowsing has widespread and long-term consequences. Whitetails suffer chronically on over-browsed habitat. Average body size decreases, fawn mortality increases, yearlings take longer to reach maturity, does have fewer twins and fewer female fawns, spikes become common and antler size declines. Until the herd is trimmed significantly and held there for years, conditions will not improve. Sometimes it's hard to cut back these beautiful animals we love to see, but in conditions like these, it is best for both animals and the land.

MIGRATION NUDGE

Hunters have long argued about what inspires deer to migrate. Some think it's snow depth; some think cold temperatures; a few suspect photo-periodism. The correct answer is yes. They're all right. Depending on the area, local traditions and even individual animals, any of the above can trigger migration.

In South Dakota's Black Hills, deer have begun migrating to lower slopes long before traditional November cold and snow hits. Some Minnesota deer were discovered heading for winter digs when the first really cold temperatures hit in November. Other deer in various parts of the country are known to leave their summer ranges only when snow gets deep enough to hinder them.

Food also affects whitetail migration. In places with nutritious, abundant forage, such as grain, whitetails hang around a week or two longer than do deer living on purely natural forage.

Some researchers have observed deer moving to summer range when weather moderated, then back to winter yards when it got nasty again. They'd also hang around near traditional yards—but not in them—until the snow really got cold and deep. This is more evidence that yards are used primarily for cover and protection from the cold, only secondarily for forage.

DROP IT, MISTER

Southern deer often carry their antlers into March, but Northern bucks dump theirs just as quickly as their testosterone fades away—usually late December or early January. Because Southern does reach estrus in late December and early January, and because they seem to drag things out longer than do Northern does, bucks remain ready and attentive at least through the first recycling period in early February. This is the equivalent of Northern bucks keeping their racks and standing at stud through early December. It's only natural, then, that this schedule would produce an antler drop in March or later.

THE TOUGH KEEP GOING

Life for Northern whitetails in winter is tough. Nature's Grim Reaper harvests the also-rans. That any deer at all can survive lying in snow night after night with temperatures below zero seems a miracle. Yet this is what they must do. Like good soldiers they march on without complaint. What choice do they have? They are what they are and they play the cards they've been dealt. And because they not only survive but thrive as one of the most beautiful, resourceful and exciting native animals, we love them all the more. These are our whitetails, our deer, symbol of everything good and strong and enduring about the wonderful American outdoors. Our first and best connection with our wilderness. May they always prosper.

Following page:
Survivor.